Learning to Solve Problems
by Searching for Macro-Operators

Richard E. Korf
Department of Computer Science, Columbia University

Learning to Solve Problems by Searching for Macro-Operators

π

Pitman Advanced Publishing Program
BOSTON · LONDON · MELBOURNE

PITMAN PUBLISHING INC
1020 Plain Street, Marshfield, Massachusetts 02050

PITMAN PUBLISHING LIMITED
128 Long Acre, London WC2E 9AN

Associated Companies
Pitman Publishing Pty Ltd, Melbourne
Pitman Publishing New Zealand Ltd, Wellington
Copp Clark Pitman, Toronto

© Richard E. Korf 1985

First published 1985

Library of Congress Cataloging in Publication Data

Korf, Richard E.
  Learning to solve problems by searching for
  macro-operators.
  Bibliography: p.
  1. Artificial intelligence.   2. Problem solving.
  I. Title.   II. Title: Macro-operators.
0335.K67   1985   001.53′5   85-3417

ISBN 0-273-08690-1

British Library Cataloguing in Publication Data

Korf, Richard E.
  Learning to solve problems by searching for macro-operators.—(Research
  notes in artificial intelligence)
  1. Problem solving
  I. Title   II. Series
  001.4′2   QA63

ISBN 0-273-08690-1

Reproduced and printed by photolithography
in Great Britain by Biddles Ltd, Guildford

Contents

Acknowledgements

This monograph is a revised version of a doctoral dissertation submitted to the Department of Computer Science at Carnegie-Mellon University. A number of people have made important contributions to this research. First and foremost is Herb Simon, my thesis advisor. His willingness to let me follow my own nose, his patience when it led me into dead ends, and his constant encouragement throughout was the most important contribution to the success of this work. Allen Newell provided many insightful critiques of this research. He raised a subtle question about the value of non-serializable subgoals that eventually led to the theory of the method. Ranan Banerji independently arrived at the basic idea behind this work. In addition, he carefully debugged the definitions, theorems, and proofs. Jon Bentley suggested the idea of interleaving the learning and problem solving components of the method. In addition, Herb, Allen, Ranan, and Jon carefully read and suggested many improvements to the manuscript. Merrick Furst exposed me to related work in group theory that provided a key contribution to this research, specifically, how to organize the macro table. Finally, I would like to thank my family, friends, and colleagues. Their moral support made this project possible.

This research was sponsored by the Defense Advanced Research Projects Agency (DOD), ARPA Order No. 3597, and monitored by the Air Force Avionics Laboratory under Contract F33615-81-K-1539.

1 Introduction and Summary

This monograph explores the idea of learning efficient strategies for solving problems by searching for *macro-operators*. A macro-operator, or *macro* for short, is simply a sequence of operators chosen from the primitive operators of a problem. The technique is particularly useful for problems with *non-serializable* subgoals, such as Rubik's Cube, for which other weak methods fail. Both a problem-solving program and a learning program are described in detail. The performance of these programs is analyzed in terms of the number of macros required to solve all problem instances, the length of the resulting solutions (expressed as the number of primitive moves), and the amount of time necessary to learn the macros. In addition, a theory of why the method works, and a characterization of the range of problems for which it is useful are presented. The theory introduces a new type of problem structure called *operator decomposability*. Finally, it is concluded that the macro technique is a valuable addition to the class of weak methods, that macro-operators constitute an interesting and important representation of knowledge, and that searching for macros may be a useful general learning paradigm.

1.1 Introduction

One view of the the field of artificial intelligence is that it is the study of *weak methods* [Newell 69]. A weak method is a general problem solving strategy that can be used when not enough knowledge about a problem is available to employ a more powerful solution technique. The virtue of the weak methods is the fact that they only require a small amount of knowledge about a problem and hence are extremely general. The set of weak methods includes generate-and-test, heuristic search, hill-climbing, and means-ends analysis. With the exception of generate and test, most of these techniques rely on a heuristic evaluation function which is used to estimate the distance to the goal. For some problems, however, no such evaluation function is known. This suggests that such problems do not have sufficient structure to employ any technique more efficient than brute-force search to solve a particular instance of the problem.[1]

Consider, however, a situation where we are not interested in solving just one instance of the problem, but rather are concerned with being able to solve many problem instances. In that case, it may be advantageous to learn a general strategy for solving any instance of the problem, and then apply it to each problem instance. This allows the computational cost of the learning stage to be amortized over all the problem instances. Such an approach will only be useful if there is some structure to the collection of problem instances such that the fixed cost of learning a single strategy plus the marginal cost of applying it to each problem instance is less than the cost of solving each instance from scratch.

In other words, even though a given instance of a problem does not have sufficient structure to allow an efficient solution, a collection of problem instances may have some common structure that allows the whole set to be solved with much less work than the sum of solving each instance individually. This suggests the existence of weak methods for learning, as opposed to problem solving, based on such structure. This work explores one such weak method of learning, that of searching for macro-operators.

1.2 Chapter Summaries

This section presents a short summary of each of the remaining chapters.

1.2.1 Chapter 2: The Need for a New Problem Solving Method

Chapter 2 demonstrates that there exist problems that have efficient solution strategies that cannot be explained by any of the current stock of weak methods, and presents a 2x2x2 version of Rubik's Cube as an example. The goal state of this problem is naturally described as a conjunction of a set of subgoals. It is observed that all known algorithms for this problem require that previously satisfied subgoals

---

[1]The terms "problem" and "problem space" in this monograph refer to a set of states and a collection of operators that connect them. A "problem instance" is a problem with a specified pair of initial and goal states.

2

be violated later in the solution path. Such a set of subgoals is referred to as *non-serializable*. However, the standard technique for solving problems with subgoals, means-ends analysis, does not allow non-serializable subgoals. Furthermore, we present empirical evidence that several natural heuristic evaluation functions for the simplified Rubik's Cube provide no useful estimate of distance to the goal, suggesting that heuristic search is of no use in solving the problem. Hence, Rubik's Cube cannot be solved by any of these techniques.

1.2.2 Chapter 3: Previous Work

Other work related to this research is reviewed in Chapter 3. Ernst and Goldstein wrote one of the first programs that learned efficient strategies for solving problems, by learning differences for the General Problem Solving program of Newell and Simon. Non-serializable subgoals were studied extensively in the context of the blocks world by Sussman, Sacerdoti, Warren, Tate, Manna and Waldinger, and others. Macro-operators were first learned and used by the STRIPS problem solver and later by the REFLECT system of Dawson and Siklossy. Banerji suggested the use of macros to deal with the non-serializable subgoals of the Rubik's Cube and the Fifteen Puzzle. Finally, Sims and others showed how to organize sets of macros to solve permutation puzzles, of which Rubik's Cube is an example, and demonstrated one way the macros could be learned.

1.2.3 Chapter 4: The Macro Problem Solver

Chapter 4 describes the *Macro Problem Solver*, an extension of the General Problem Solver to include macro-operators. The basic idea of the method is to apply macros that may temporarily violate previously satisfied subgoals within their application, but that restore all previous subgoals to their satisfied states by the end of the macro, and satisfy an additional subgoal as well. The macros are stored in a two dimensional table, called a *macro table*, in which each column of the table contains the macros necessary to satisfy a particular subgoal. The subgoals are solved one at a time, by applying a single macro from each column of the table. The Macro Problem Solver generates very efficient solutions to several classical problems, some of which cannot be handled by other weak methods. The examples include Rubik's Cube, the Eight and Fifteen Puzzles, the Think-a-Dot problem, and the Towers of Hanoi problem.

1.2.4 Chapter 5: Learning Macro-Operators

The question of how macros are learned or acquired is the subject of Chapter 5. The simplest technique is a brute-force search. However, by using a technique related to bidirectional search, the depth of the search can be cut in half. Finally, existing macros can be composed to find macros that are beyond the search limits. These techniques are sufficient for learning the necessary set of macros for the example problems. In addition, a design for a general *Macro Learning Program* is presented. The design clearly separates the problem-dependent components of the method from the problem-independent features. A key property of the learning program is that *all* the macros necessary to solve *any* problem instance are found in a *single* search from the goal state.

1.2.5 Chapter 6: The Theory of Macro Problem Solving

Chapter 6 explains the theory of macro problem solving and characterizes the range of problems for which it is effective. The theory is presented in two parts: a special case in which a state is represented by a vector of state variables, and the general theory that encompasses arbitrary state representations. A necessary and sufficient condition for the success of the method is a new type of problem structure called *operator decomposability*. A totally decomposable operator is one that may affect more than one state variable, but whose effect can be decomposed into its effect on each state variable independently. The degree of operator decomposability in a problem constrains the ordering of the subgoals, ranging from complete freedom in the case of Rubik's Cube, to a total ordering for the Towers of Hanoi problem. In addition, further generalizations of the method are presented. For example, we show that in some cases, efficient solution strategies can be learned based on randomly generated subgoals!

1.2.6 Chapter 7: Performance Analysis

An analysis of the performance of the problem solving and learning programs is presented in Chapter 7. The performance measures include the number of macros that must be stored for a given problem, the amount of time required to learn the macros, and the length of solutions generated in terms of number of primitive moves, both in the worst case and the average case. The first result is that the total number of macros is the sum of the number of macros in each column whereas the number of states in the space is the product of these values. The total learning time for the macros is shown to be of the same order as the amount of time required to find a solution to a single problem instance without the macros. Finally, if there are N subgoals to a problem, the solution length generated by the Macro Problem Solver is less than or equal to N times the optimal solution length, in the worst case. In addition, an average case analysis of solution length is found to agree with experimental results for the 2x2x2 Rubik's Cube. Furthermore, for the Eight Puzzle and the full 3x3x3 Rubik's Cube, the solution lengths generated by the Macro Problem Solver are close to or shorter than those of an average human problem solver. An important feature of this analysis is that each performance parameter is expressed in terms of a corresponding measure of problem *difficulty*, rather than problem *size*. For example, the worst-case solution length is expressed in terms of the optimal solution length.

1.2.7 Chapter 8: Reflections and Further Work

Several observations and directions for future research are presented in Chapter 8. First, the selection of subgoals and their ordering are two parameters of the Macro Learning Program whose automatic generation requires further research. Next, we show that the Macro Problem Solver can be combined effectively with other problem solving methods such as operator subgoaling, macro generalization, and problem decomposition, to solve problems that no single technique could solve alone. In addition, we argue that given an ordered set of subgoals for a problem, the difficulty of the problem is related to the maximum distance between two successive subgoals, in terms of number of primitive moves. Next, we propose that macro-operators are an important representation for knowledge, based on a brief look at the domains of theorem proving and computer programming, and a detailed examination of the domain of road navigation. Finally, an exploration of the utility of macros in arbitrary problem spaces suggests that searching for macro-operators may be a fairly general learning paradigm.

1.2.8 Chapter 9: Conclusions

Chapter 9 presents the conclusions of this research. They include the finding that the macro learning and problem solving techniques constitute a valuable addition to the collection of weak methods, the idea that macro-operators are an important representation for knowledge, and the suggestion that searching for macros may be a useful paradigm for learning.

2 The Need for a New Problem Solving Method

The purpose of this chapter is to demonstrate that the existing collection of weak methods is incomplete. There exists a problem, namely Rubik's Cube, that cannot be solved efficiently by any of the current stock of weak methods. Yet, people can solve it, and even learn to solve it, quite efficiently. Hence, another method must underly the solution of this problem. In addition, we will argue that for other reasons as well, Rubik's Cube is an excellent domain for studying problem solving and learning.

2.1 Problem Description: 2x2x2 Rubik's Cube

Figure 2-1 shows a 2x2x2 version of the celebrated Rubik's Cube, invented by Erno Rubik in 1975. The puzzle is a cube that is cut by three planes, one normal to each axis, separating it into eight subcubes, referred to as *cubies*[1]. The four cubies on either side of each cutting plane can be rotated in either direction with respect to the other four cubies. Note that these rotations, called *twists*, can be made along each of the three axes. The twists can be 90 degrees in either direction or 180 degrees.

Each of the cubies has three sides facing out, called *facelets*, each a different color. In the goal state of the puzzle, the four facelets on each side of the cube are all the same color, making six different colors in all, one for each side of the cube. The cube is initialized by performing an arbitrary series of twists to mix the colors on each side. The problem then is to *solve* the cube, or find a sequence of twists that will restore the cube to the goal state, i.e. each side showing a single color.

The 2x2x2 cube is a simpler version of Rubik's original cube. The original is a

---

[1]The terminology used here is standard in the literature of Rubik's Cube [Frey 82].

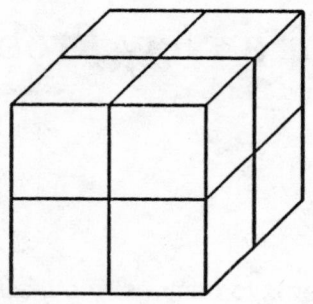

Figure 2-1: 2x2x2 Rubik's Cube

3x3x3 cube with two planes of rotation cutting each axis (see Figure 2-2). The 2x2x2 cube is a subproblem of the 3x3x3 cube: it is isomorphic to a restriction of the full cube in which only the eight cubies on the corners are considered. In other words, if one ignores the interior edge and center cubies of the 3x3x3 cube, then the problem reduces to the 2x2x2 cube. Both problems will be considered in this work.

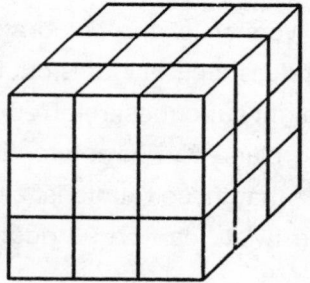

Figure 2-2: 3x3x3 Rubik's Cube

2.2 Rubik's Cube as a Domain for Problem Solving and Learning Research

There are several reasons why Rubik's Cube is an excellent domain for research on problem solving and particularly on learning problem solving strategies.

First, note that there are two levels of tasks associated with the cube. One is the task of given a particular initial configuration, find a sequence of twists that will restore it to the goal state. This is the problem solving task. The other is the learning task of acquiring a strategy that will solve the cube from any initial state. The reason for this distinction is that the puzzle is really a collection of a very large number of problem instances, one for each possible initial state[2].

An obvious reason for studying Rubik's cube is that the problem is well structured yet very difficult. Since the states and operators are clearly specified and easily represented, one can easily construct a problem space for the problem. That the problem is genuinely difficult is attested to by the phenomenally large number of people who have unsuccessfully worked on scrambled cubes. The published strategies to the problem are all fairly complex in the sense that it is considered a significant achievement to learn one of them. Furthermore, the problem of discovering a strategy is even more difficult. Most people who try it never succeed, and those who do succeed typically require several weeks to several months of effort.

Not only does it take a long time to learn a strategy, but progress toward it is incremental and observable. Many problems are difficult and require a long time to solve, but the solution, once discovered, becomes apparent instantaneously. In Rubik's Cube, progress toward a strategy occurs throughout the learning process and can be measured in terms of the number of cubies that can be correctly positioned relative to the goal state. In addition, it is usually clear what pieces of knowledge are being acquired during the learning. These features of the problem make it an ideal domain for studying the learning of problem solving strategies.

Finally, the most compelling reason for studying Rubik's Cube is the fact that it cannot be solved efficiently by any of the current stock of weak methods. After describing a problem space for the 2x2x2 cube, evidence supporting this claim will be presented.

---

[2]The term "solution" is used to refer to a sequence of primitive moves that maps a particular initial state to a particular goal state. The term "strategy" refers to an algorithm that will generate a solution to any problem instance.

2.3 Problem Space

This section presents a problem space for the 2x2x2 cube by describing a data structure to represent a state or configuration of the cube, and giving a procedural implementation of each of the primitive operators of the puzzle. In general, the task of going from a problem description to a representation of the problem is complex, and if done cleverly can result in a vast reduction in problem solving effort. In this case, however, the representation is based on relatively straightforward observations and does not significantly reduce the difficulty of the problem.

2.3.1 State Representation

The primary issue in generating a problem space for any problem is designing a data structure to represent a state of the problem. Perhaps the most obvious state representation would be to list in some order the colors that appear on each facelet of the cube. However, the choice of a facelet as a primitive results in an inefficient representation. The reason is that the facelets are physically constrained to occur in fixed groups of three by virtue of being attached to particular cubies, which move as units. Incorporating this constraint directly in the representation gives rise to a more efficient representation.

By choosing a cubie as the primitive of the representation, we are led to represent a cube configuration as a permutation of the cubies among the different positions, or *cubicles*, that the cubies can occupy. In addition, a particular cubie can exist in the same position but with its colors twisted in any of three different orientations, one corresponding to each facelet of the cubie. The three orientations will be labelled 0, 1, and 2. The orientation is determined by examining the unique facelet of each cubie that faces either up or down in the goal state of the cube. Its orientation is the number of 120 degree clockwise rotations of the cubie about an axis from the center of the cube through the corner of the cubie which would map the up or down facelet from the top or bottom side of the cube to its current position.

Thus, each cubie must be represented by both its position and its orientation. This suggests an eight element array of cubies, where each element encodes both

10

the position and the orientation of the cubie. Note that there also exists a dual representation where each element corresponds to a cubicle and the value encodes the cubie that occupies it along with its orientation. However, the former will be used throughout.

For economy, we do not want to consider states that differ only by a simple rotation of the entire cube as different. This is accomplished by defining a canonical orientation of the cube. A canonical orientation is obtained by picking a particular cubie and fixing its position and orientation. Each operator can then be viewed as a twist followed by a rotation of the entire cube to restore the fixed cubie to its canonical position and orientation. Another way of looking at this is that since each twist rotates half the cubies with respect to the other half, either half can be viewed as fixed and the other half as rotating. When all three planes of rotation are considered, a single cubie can be considered as permanently fixed. In either case, the effect is that only seven cubies are movable, and only three faces can be twisted, without loss of generality.

The cubies have three letter names which represent the three planes which intersect at the goal position of the cubie. The planes are labelled Up, Down, Left, Right, Front, and Back. Hence, the complete set of cubies is {ULF, ULB, URF, URB, DLF, DLB, DRF, DRB}, with DLB being the fixed cubie.

2.3.2 Operator Implementation

Given a representation of the state of the cube, an implementation of the twists or operators of the cube are easily derived. Each individual operator is represented by an array of 21 elements, one for each possible combination of seven cubicles and three orientations for a cubie. The value of a particular element encodes the position and orientation that a cubie would be mapped to by that operator, given that it was in the position and orientation that corresponds to the array element. In other words, the operator array serves as a mapping function from the previous values of the cubies to the values resulting from the operator application. To apply an operator, the values of each of the seven cubies must be mapped to their new values. Note that cubies occupying cubicles that are unaffected by a particular operator will remain unchanged. There is a separate operator array for each individual operator. Since there are three faces to be twisted, and each face can be twisted 90 degrees clockwise, 90 degrees counterclockwise, or 180 degrees, there are nine primitive operators in all. They are labelled by the first letter of the plane that they rotate. By convention, a 90 degree clockwise twist of a plane is represented simply by the first letter of the plane, a 90 degree counterclockwise twist is indicated by the letter followed by a minus sign, and a 180 degree twist by the letter followed by a 2. The complete set of primitive moves for the 2x2x2 cube is thus {U, U-, U2, R, R-, R2, F, F-, F2}.

Table 2-1 shows the effect of each operator on the positions of cubies, while Table 2-2 shows the effect of the operators on the orientation of the cubies. Note that twists of the Up face leave orientation invariant. Similarly, 180 degree twists do not effect orientation. The effect of the remaining operators on orientation depends on the initial position of the cubie.

Table 2-1: Effect of operators on positions of cubies for 2x2x2 Rubik's Cube

OPERATOR	EFFECT			
U	URF>ULF,	ULF>ULB,	ULB>URB,	URB>URF
U2	URF>ULB,	ULF>URB,	ULB>URF,	URB>ULF
U-	URF>URB,	ULF>URF,	ULB>ULF,	URB>ULB
R	URF>URB,	URB>DRB,	DRF>URF,	DRB>DRF
R2	URF>DRB,	URB>DRF,	DRF>URB,	DRB>URF
R-	URF>DRF,	URB>URF,	DRF>DRB,	DRB>URB
F	URF>DRF,	ULF>URF,	DLF>ULF,	DRF>DLF
F2	URF>DLF,	ULF>DRF,	DLF>URF,	DRF>ULF
F-	URF>ULF,	ULF>DLF,	DLF>DRF,	DRF>URF

Table 2-2: Effect of operators on orientation of cubies for 2x2x2 Rubik's Cube

OPERATOR	INITIAL POSITION	EFFECT		
R	URF or DRB	0>1,	1>2,	2>0
R	URB or DRF	0>2,	1>0,	2>1
R-	URF or DRB	0>1,	1>2,	2>0
R-	URB or DRF	0>2,	1>0,	2>1
F	URF or DLF	0>2,	1>0,	2>1
F	ULF or DRF	0>1,	1>2,	2>0
F-	URF or DLF	0>2,	1>0,	2>1
F-	ULF or DRF	0>1,	1>2,	2>0

2.4 Brute Force Search

Given a problem space for Rubik's Cube, we could solve it using brute force search. We would expect a breadth-first search to look at about half the states in the space, on the average, before finding a solution.

The 2x2x2 cube has 3,674,160 distinct states. This number comes from the product of 7!, for the permutations of the cubie positions, with 3^7, for the orientations of the cubies. This value is then divided by three because the total state space is composed of three different, disconnected components. Thus, brute force search is impractical for a human, but is quite practical for a computer.

However, when we consider the 3x3x3 Rubik's Cube, the number of states grows to approximately $4*10^{19}$. Even at a million twists per second, it would take a computer an average of 700,000 years to solve the cube with brute force search. Hence, another technique must be used.

2.5 Means-Ends Analysis

Note that the goal state of Rubik's Cube is naturally expressed as a conjunction of subgoals such as "get the colors on each face to match", or "get each cubie to its correct position and orientation." This suggests setting up a sequence of subgoals and using means-ends analysis to solve them one at a time. The General Problem Solving (GPS) program of Newell and Simon [Newell 72] implements means-ends analysis, in conjunction with with other problem solving techniques such as operator subgoaling. A necessary condition for its applicability is that there exist a set of subgoals and an ordering among them, such that once a subgoal is satisfied, it need never be violated in order to satisfy the remaining subgoals [Ernst 69]. A set of subgoals with this property is called *serializable*.

Unfortunately, Rubik's Cube does not satisfy this condition. A few minutes of experimentation with the cube reveals the aspect of the problem that makes it so difficult and frustrating. In particular, once some of the cubies are put into place, in general they must be "messed up" in order to position the remaining cubies correctly. All of the published solutions to the problem, of which there are many, share this feature of violating previously solved subgoals, at least temporarily, in order to solve additional subgoals.

To be precise, there are several technical qualifications that must be attached to the claim that Rubik's Cube does not satisfy the applicability condition for GPS. One is that for the degenerate case where we assume only a single subgoal which is the main goal, the condition is vacuously satisfied: once this subgoal is satisfied, it need not be violated in order to satisfy the main goal. Unfortunately, this formulation makes no contribution to the solution of the problem.

A more interesting caveat is that there exists a relatively long sequence of subgoals that do satisfy the GPS condition. First, we partition the complete set of states into the set of states that are a minimum of one move from the goal, the states that are a minimum of two moves from the goal, three moves, etc. The subgoals are then of the form, "move from the current state to a state which is one move closer to the goal." These subgoals are well defined and can be solved sequentially without ever violating a previous subgoal. The difficulty is that we don't have any method for computing these sets other than brute force search, and even if we could compute them, we don't have any more economical representation of them than an exhaustive table.

Hence, we must modify our claim to say that means-ends analysis, in its current form, offers no practical benefit for solving Rubik's Cube.

2.6 Heuristic Search

Even though we do not have a set of serializable subgoals, there may be a heuristic evaluation function that, though not guaranteed to vary monotonically toward the goal, may nevertheless offer a useful estimate of problem solving progress. A heuristic evaluation function is a function that is relatively cheap to compute from a given state, and that provides an estimate of the distance from that state to the goal. Most of the weak methods except for generate and test (which provides no problem solving power) rely on such a function, either explicitly or implicitly. For example, the evaluation function is the essence of simple heuristic search. Hill-climbing requires an evaluation function that, in addition, must be

14

monotonic. If we view the number of subgoals remaining to be satisfied as an evaluation function, then even means-ends analysis uses an evaluation function, which must be monotonic as well.

The usefulness of an evaluation function is directly related to its accuracy in estimating the distance to the goal. In an effort to find a useful heuristic for Rubik's Cube, several plausible candidates were tested experimentally to determine their accuracy. The surprising results were that none of the heuristics tested produced values that had any correlation at all with distance from the goal!

The basic idea of the experiment is to compute the average distance from the goal state for all the states that produce a particular value of a given evaluation function. The 2x2x2 Rubik's Cube was used to allow every state of the problem space to be evaluated. The first step of the experiment was to conduct a breadth-first search of the entire space, generating a table which lists the minimum distance of each state to the goal state. The maximum distance of any state from the goal is 11 moves, and the average distance over all states is 8.76 moves.

The next step was to identify plausible evaluation functions, which resulted in four fairly obvious ones. The first heuristic function is simply the number of cubies that are in their goal positions and orientations. Considering position and orientation independently, the second function awards one point for a cubie in its goal position, one point for a cubie in its goal orientation, and two points for both. Reasoning that the position of a cubie relative to its neighbors in the goal state is more important than absolute position, the next heuristic counts the number of pairs of adjacent cubies that are in the correct position and orientation relative to each other, without regard to their global position or orientation. Taking into account the distance of a cubie from its goal position, the final evaluation function determines the minimum number of moves required to correctly position and orient each cubie independently, and sums these values over all the cubies.

The results of the experiments are presented as a set of graphs, one for each evaluation function (see Figures 2-3 through 2-6). In each case, the x-axis of the graph corresponds to the different values produced by the function. The y-axis of the graph corresponds to the actual distance from the goal state. Each data point gives the average distance from the goal state for the set of states which produce a particular value of the evaluation function.

The results show that in general, the average distance from the goal of a set of states sharing a particular heuristic value is within 10% of 8.76, the average for the entire state space. This result holds across almost all values of all the evaluation functions. The only significant deviation from this norm is that the states whose evaluations are closest to that of the goal state are in fact further from the goal than the average state! However, none of the evaluation functions identify a set of states that are even a single move closer to the goal state, on the average.

This implies that none of the above heuristics are of any direct use in solving the 2x2x2 Rubik's Cube. Attempts to use these heuristics to reduce the amount of search required for the 3x3x3 cube were unsuccessful as well. Since these heuristics were the best we could come up with, we may conclude that if there does exist a useful heuristic, its form is probably quite complex, the limiting case being the heuristic of moving one step closer to the goal. Furthermore, none of the literature on the cube suggests any other evaluation functions. All this evidence suggests that heuristic evaluation functions are not in fact used to solve this problem.

2.7 Conclusion

Rubik's Cube is an example of a problem that cannot be solved efficiently by any of our current problem solving methods, including means-ends analysis and heuristic search, yet can be solved efficiently by people. Hence, another method must be involved. The elucidation and analysis of that method is the subject of this monograph.

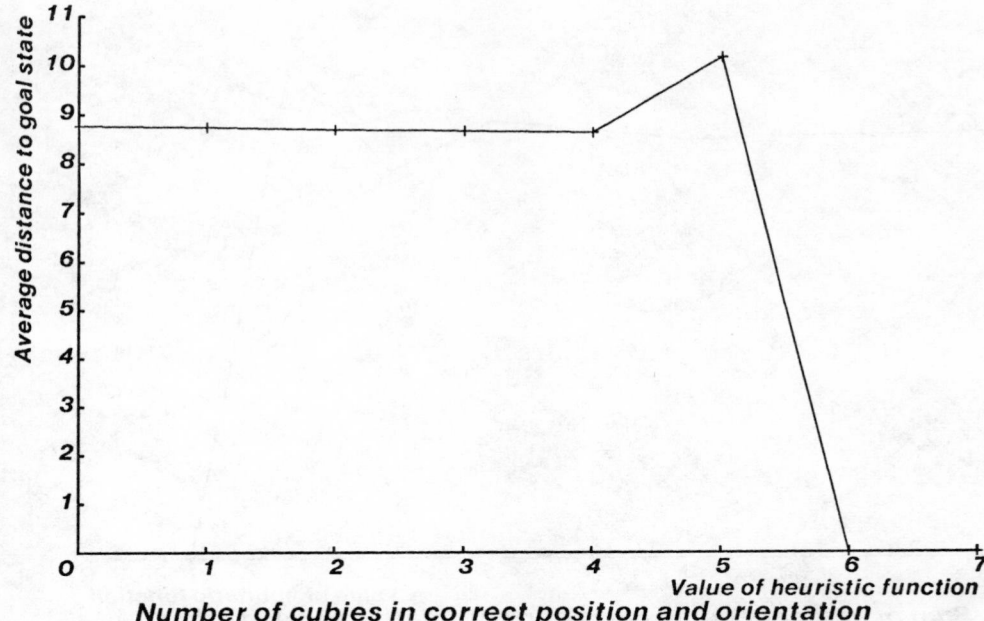

Figure 2-3: Average distance to goal state vs. number of cubies in correct
position and orientation

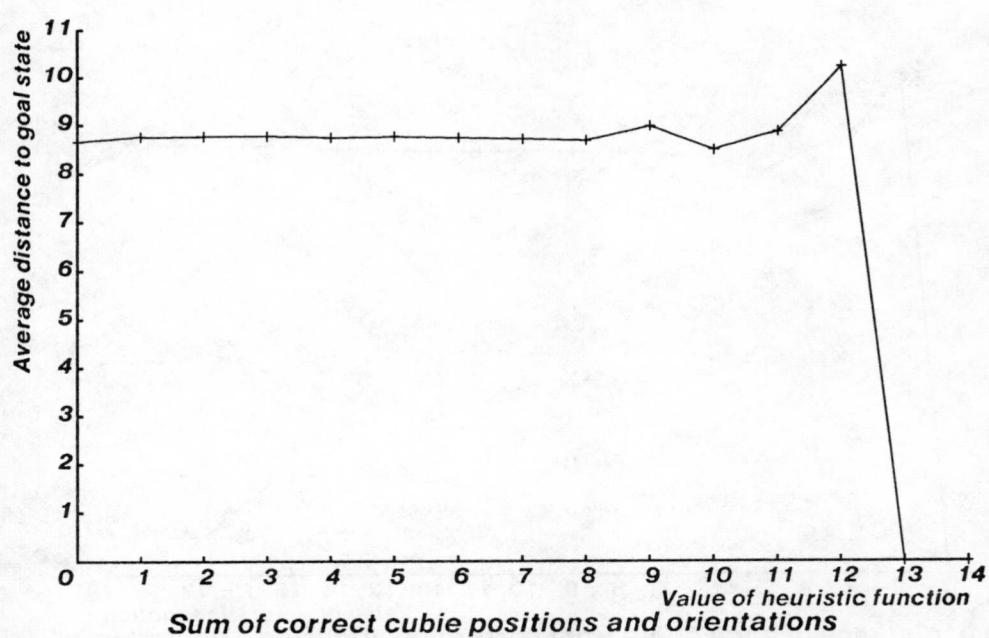

Figure 2-4: Average distance to goal state vs. sum of correct cubie positions
and orientations

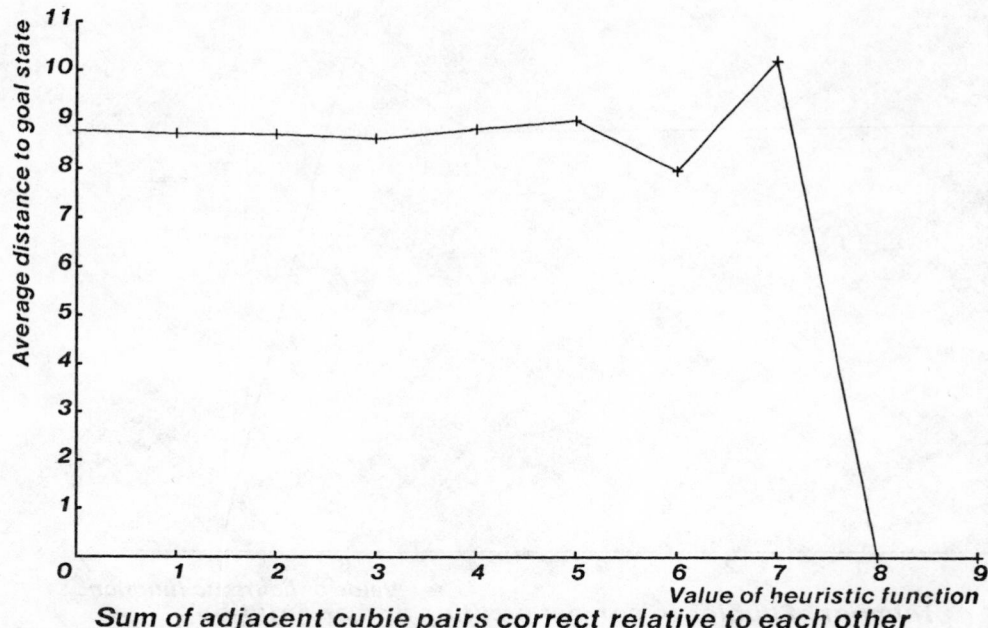

Figure 2-5: Average distance to goal state vs. sum of adjacent cubie pairs correct relative to each other

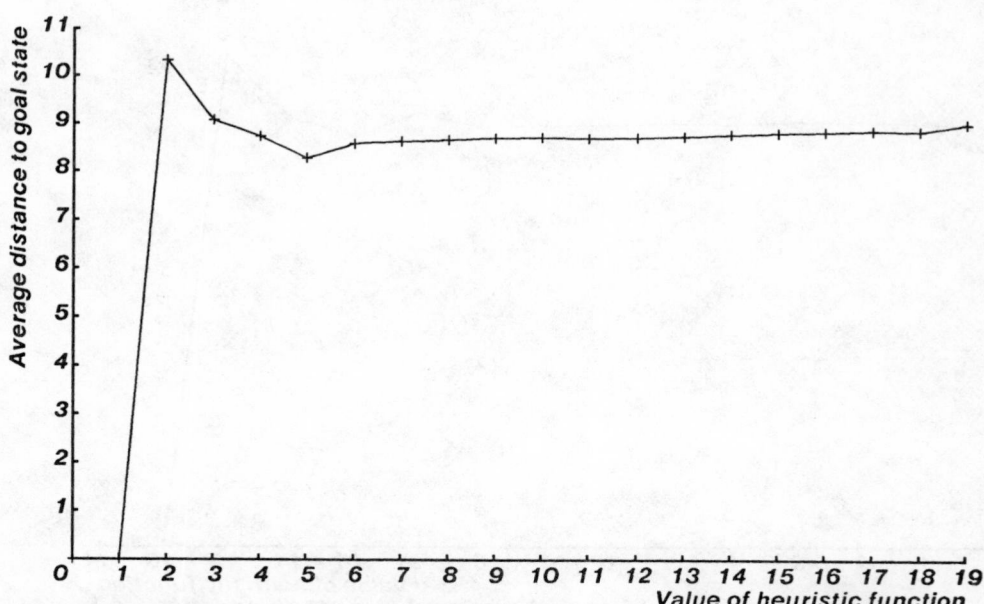

Figure 2-6: Average distance to goal state vs. sum of distance of each cubie from correct position and orientation

3 Previous Work

This chapter reviews previous work that has contributed to or is related to the development of the Macro Problem Solver. It includes work on changing representations in problem solving, GPS and the work of Ernst and Goldstein on learning differences, research on non-serializable subgoals in the context of the blocks world, the development of the idea of macro-operators, the ideas of Banerji for using macros to deal with non-serializable subgoals, and work on permutation groups.

3.1 Change of Representation

The present work originated in attempts to understand the process of changing representations in problem solving [Korf 80]. The reason for changing the representation of a problem is to find a more efficient strategy for solving the problem. The goal of this research was to take a given representation for a problem, and automatically construct a new representation in which problem solving is more efficient. It was found that two types of representation changes that produce large efficiency gains are the identification of useful differences or subgoals in the space, and the addition of macro-operators to the set of primitive operators. In these contexts, the problem of automatically deriving improved representations becomes one of learning good differences or of acquiring useful macros.

3.2 Learning Differences for GPS

Included in the work of Ernst and Goldstein on "Mechanical discovery of classes of problem solving strategies" [Ernst 82] is an approach to learning subgoals. Ernst and Goldstein investigated two different types of problem solving strategies: the General Problem Solver of Newell and Simon [Newell 72], and strategies for playing two-person games similar to Nim. We will restrict our attention to the GPS component of their work.

As described in the previous chapter, GPS solves a problem by using an ordered set of differences and removing them one at a time, such that the main goal can be reached without reintroducing a previously removed difference. The original version of GPS required that the differences and their ordering be provided by the user in the form of a difference table. The contribution of Ernst and Goldstein was to show that these difference tables could be discovered automatically for a range of problems for which good differences are known, effectively learning an efficient strategy for the problem within the GPS paradigm.

An important feature of Ernst and Goldstein's program is that it is able to construct complex, non-obvious differences for problems. For example, consider the Fools Disk problem (see Figure 3-1) which consists of four concentric disks with eight numbers evenly spaced around each disk. Each of the disks can be rotated independently, and the goal state of the problem is one in which each of the eight radial rows of four numbers sum to 12. The obvious subgoals of getting the radii to sum to 12 one at a time are not serializable, regardless of their ordering. Hence, Goldstein's program constructs a more complex series of three subgoals: first get the sixteen numbers on the horizontal and vertical radii to sum to 48, which implies that the sum of the diagonal radii also must sum to 48, then get each of the four diameters to sum to 24, and then finally get each radius to sum to 12. In order to make these subgoals serializable, after the first subgoal is achieved, only 90 degree rotations of the disks are allowed, since these moves leave invariant the total sum of the horizontal and vertical radii. Similarly, after the second subgoal is achieved, only 180 degree rotations are considered, since these moves leave the sums of the diameters invariant. Thus, these subgoals are both serializable and effective for solving the problem. It is interesting to note that if the problem is formulated with only 45 degree rotations as primitive operators, then the 90 and 180 degree rotations in this strategy become macro-operators.

The development of the Macro Problem Solver owes several intellectual debts to GPS and to Ernst and Goldstein's work. Its structure borrows heavily from that of GPS, to the extent that the Macro Problem Solver is actually a generalization of GPS to include macro-operators in addition to primitive operators. In addition, the work of Ernst and Goldstein provided the paradigm of learning by the discovery of

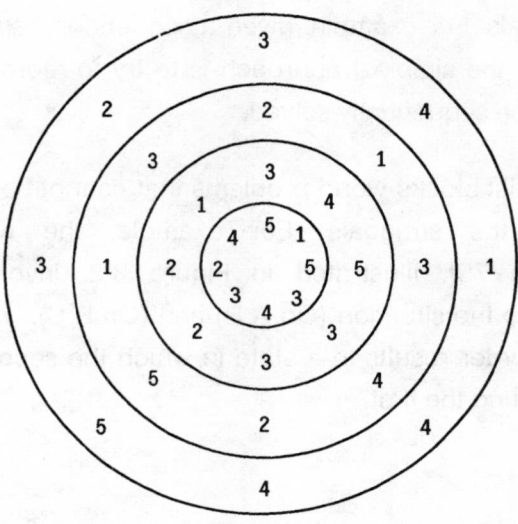

Figure 3-1: Fool's Disk problem

parameters to a particular problem solving method, a paradigm that is followed in the learning of macros. Finally, the observation that the Eight Puzzle was not included as one of Ernst and Goldstein's examples, and the conclusion that no good set of GPS differences existed for that problem, provided the original motivation for investigating the class of problems for which GPS is not applicable. In fact, the one problem that Ernst and Goldstein's program was unsuccessful in finding good differences for, the Think-A-Dot problem, is included as one of the Macro Problem Solver examples in the next chapter.

3.3 Non-Serializable Subgoals

The problem of non-serializable subgoals was studied in the context of the blocks world by a number of researchers in the early 1970s. Sussman's HACKER program [Sussman 75] deals with problems of building stacks of blocks represented by sets of conjunctive subgoals of the form (On X Y), where X and Y are blocks. There are two operators that can be applied: (Cleartop X), which removes all blocks from the top of block X, and (Puton X Y), which places block X directly on top of block Y, assuming both their tops are clear. HACKER works by initially assuming that the subgoals can be achieved independently and then explicitly invoking a set of "debugging" mechanisms to deal with interactions between the subgoals. For example, given a sequence of subgoals that cannot be solved sequentially, the simplest approach is to try to reorder the subgoals into a sequence that can be sequentially solved.

However, there exist blocks-world problems that cannot be solved sequentially by any ordering of the subgoals. For example, the well-known "Sussman Anomaly" [Sussman 75], illustrated in Figure 3-2, involves transforming the situation (On C A) to the situation (On A B) and (On B C). Attempting to solve the subgoals in either order results in a state in which the second subgoal cannot be solved without violating the first.

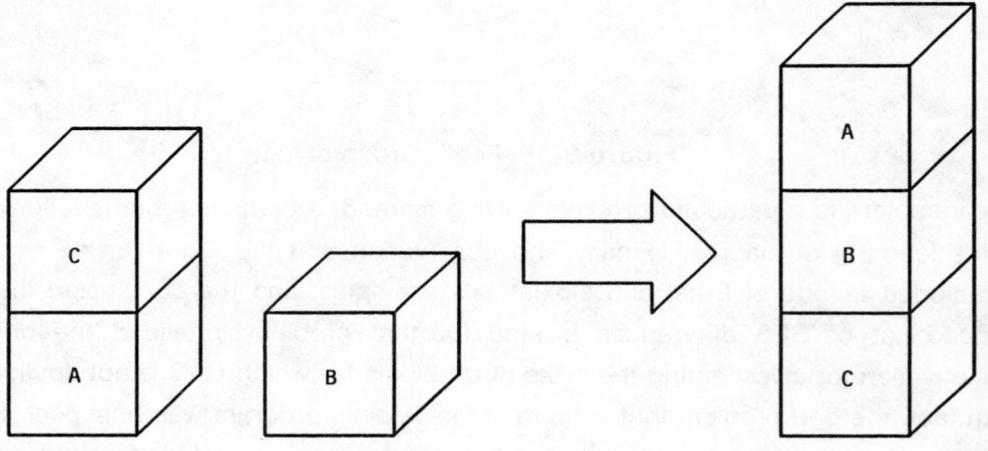

Figure 3-2: Sussman Anomaly

Sussman's HACKER can solve this problem only by running in an anomalous mode in which subgoals are not protected. Furthermore, the result is a non-optimal solution such as: (Cleartop A), (Puton A B), (Cleartop B), (Puton B C), and (Puton A B), whereas an optimal solution is: (Cleartop A), (Puton B C), and (Puton A B).

Shortly after Sussman's work, Warren, Tate, and Waldinger all arrived at essentially the same technique for generating optimal plans for such problems. Warren [Warren 74] noted that the key to the optimal solution to the Sussman Anomaly is that the action that solves the second subgoal occurs between the two actions that solve the first subgoal. Tate's system [Tate 75] potentially reorders all the subgoals generated to solve a problem, including subgoals to satisfy operator preconditions, as opposed to just the top level subgoals. Waldinger [Waldinger 81], working in the domain of program synthesis, generates a plan to solve one subgoal and then insert actions within the body of the plan to solve successive subgoals without violating previous subgoals. Sacerdoti [Sacerdoti 75] generalizes these approaches to represent a plan as a partial order of actions and uses the principle of least commitment to avoid problems caused by arbitrary ordering of the actions.

There are several limitations to this body of work in dealing with non-serializable subgoals. One is that most of these systems, with the exception of that of Manna and Waldinger, simply reorder the primitive actions necessary to achieve each of the subgoals independently, without the capability of adding new actions to deal directly with subgoal interactions [Sacerdoti 75]. A second limitation is that these techniques only work on problems for which independence of subgoals is a good first approximation [Sussman 75]. Finally, we note that the subgoal interaction in the blocks world is not an inherent property of the domain but rather an artifact of the particular subgoals chosen to decompose a goal. In particular, if we simply add a subgoal of the form (On X Table) where X is the bottom-most block of a stack, then all the block stacking problems could be solved by GPS simply by first putting the bottom block on the table, then the next higher block, and so on until the top block is placed on top of the stack. For these reasons, it seems unlikely that these methods would be powerful enough to deal with the complexity of subgoal interactions manifested by Rubik's Cube.

3.4 Macro-Operators

The idea of composing a sequence of primitive operators and viewing the sequence as a single operator goes back as least as far as Saul Amarel's 1968 paper on representations for the Missionaries and Cannibals problem [Amarel 68]. He notes that the introduction of macros drastically reduces the effective size of the search space, resulting in a solution with practically no search. He also notes the analogy between macros in a problem space and well-chosen lemmas in a mathematical system.

The first implementation of this idea is the use of MACROPS [Fikes 72] in the

STRIPS problem solver. The main contributions of this work with respect to macros are the powerful mechanisms for generalizing macros. In particular, macros can be parameterized by replacing constant arguments with variables, and are stored in a form that allows arbitrary subsequences of a macro to be applied.

There are several features of the work on MACROPS that distinguish it from the research reported here. The most important is that MACROPS are not used to overcome the problems of non-serializable subgoals but rather to improve the efficiency of the STRIPS problem solver in a domain for which there exists a good set of GPS differences. The robot problem solving domain of STRIPS consists of a robot and a set of boxes distributed among a collection of connected rooms, and poses problems of moving boxes between rooms. Like the blocks world, an effective set of ordered subgoals can be set up for these problems. For example, first move the robot to the room containing the box to be moved, then move the box to its destination, and finally move the robot to its final destination. In fact, by using such a set of serializable subgoals, the LAWALY system of Siklossy and Druessi [Siklossy 73] was able to solve the same problems more than an order of magnitude faster than STRIPS with MACROPS. The fact that STRIPS with MACROPS performs so inefficiently in this simple domain suggests that the system is not powerful enough to handle more complex domains.

A second limitation of STRIPS with MACROPS is that it does not generate a complete set of macros. MACROPS are generated by using the solutions to particular problems posed to the system, and serve to reduce but not eliminate the amount of search required on future problems. The questions of what problems to use in a training sequence, and how much search is still required to solve problems chosen from some population given a set of MACROPS, are difficult and left unanswered. By contrast, the Macro Problem Solver works from a complete set of macros that eliminate search entirely.

The idea of separating a learning stage for acquiring macros from the problem solving phase is implemented in the REFLECT system of Dawson and Siklossy [Dawson 77]. Their system has a preprocessing stage where macro-operators, called BIGOPS, are generated by comparing the postconditions of each primitive operator with the preconditions of all possible successor operators,

24

creating a two-operator macro whenever they match. This results in a relatively small set of macros which are independent of any particular problems to be solved. Unfortunately, this approach is limited to very short macros or to operator sets where the preconditions severely constrain the possible operator sequences.

3.5 Macros and Non-Serializable Subgoals

The fact that macro-operators can be used to overcome the problem of non-serializable subgoals was first suggested by Banerji [Banerji 83]. He points out that both Rubik's Cube and the Fifteen Puzzle cannot be solved by a straightforward application of GPS, but that an extension of GPS to include macros would be able to solve these problems. For example, in both the Eight and Fifteen Puzzles, when the next to last tile in a row is correctly placed, in general it must be moved in order to place the last tile in that row, hence violating a previously satisfied subgoal. Banerji suggests that at a given stage of a strategy, the macros that are useful are ones that leave all previously satisfied subgoals intact while satisfying an additional subgoal as well. He also notes that within the body of a macro, a previous subgoal may be violated, but by the end of the macro, the subgoal must be restored. Banerji's work was independent of and concurrent with this research.

3.6 Permutation Groups

Given that macros may be useful for solving problems with non-serializable subgoals, the issue of exactly what macros are necessary and how to use them in an efficient strategy must be addressed. A solution to this problem is suggested by the work of Sims [Sims 70] on computational problems of permutation groups. The goal of that research, and related work by others, is to be able to represent a permutation group compactly so that questions such as the order of the group and membership in the group can be answered efficiently.

A permutation group of degree n is a subset, not necessarily proper, of all permutations of n elements which is closed under the operation of composition. For example, consider Rubik's Cube and define two macro-operators to be equivalent if and only if both macros have the same effect on all states. Then, since each macro permutes the positions and orientations of the cubies, and any macro can be composed with any other to yield another macro, the collection of equivalence classes of macros for Rubik's Cube form a permutation group. The representation for permutation groups proposed by Sims is an $n \times n$ matrix of permutations. Table 3-1 shows an example of such a matrix for the permutation group on 5 elements. All the permutations in the ith column of the matrix leave the first $i - 1$ elements of the permutation invariant. The permutation in the jth row of the ith column maps the jth element to the ith position.

Table 3-1: Permutation matrix for permutation group on 5 elements.

	1	2	3	4	5
1	(1 2 3 4 5)				
2	(2 1 3 4 5)	(1 2 3 4 5)			
3	(3 1 2 4 5)	(1 3 2 4 5)	(1 2 3 4 5)		
4	(4 1 2 3 5)	(1 4 2 3 5)	(1 2 4 3 5)	(1 2 3 4 5)	
5	(5 1 2 3 4)	(1 5 2 3 4)	(1 2 5 3 4)	(1 2 3 5 4)	(1 2 3 4 5)

Sims also addresses the issue of how to compute these permutations, given a set of generators of the group, or primitive permutations. The technique relies on the observation that if permutation **A** leaves the first $i - 1$ elements invariant and maps the jth element to the ith position, and permutation **B** has the same property, then **A** composed with the inverse of **B** will leave the first i elements invariant. Using this fact, Sims implemented an algorithm to fill in the permutation table. Furst, Hopcroft, and Luks [Furst 80] later showed that the complexity of a similar algorithm is a polynomial of order n^6 where n is the number of elements permuted. Knuth[1] reduced this upper bound to $n^5 \log n$, and Jerrum [Jerrum 82] further reduced it to n^5 for a slightly different representation.

As we will see in the next chapter, replacing the permutations in such a table with corresponding sequences of primitive operators gives rise to an effective strategy for solving permutation problems. There are two limitations, however, to this work from the point of view of general problem solving. One is that it refers only to

---

[1] personal communication from Donald Knuth to Eugene Luks, May 1981.

permutation groups and must be extended to apply to a broader class of problems. For example, even though the states of the Eight Puzzle are permutations of the tiles, the operator sequences of the problem do not form a group because arbitrary operator sequences cannot be composed. The reason is that the position of the blank at the end of the first sequence must match the position of the blank required at the start of the second. Similarly, preconditions on the operators in the Towers of Hanoi problem preclude the composition of arbitrary operator sequences. In the case of the Think-a-Dot problem, there are no operator preconditions, and the problem does form a permutation group, but only in the sense that the operators permute the states of the problem. The Sims representation is worthless for this problem since the size of the table is $O(n^2)$ where n is the number of elements being permuted. Thus, the representation is only useful when the number of elements to be permuted is small relative to the number of states in the problem space.

The second limitation of this work is that the technique used to fill in the permutation table results in extremely inefficient solutions, relative to human strategies, in terms of number of primitive moves. In general, the permutations in a particular column of the table are produced by composing two permutations from the previous column. If we replace permutations by macros, this doubles the length of the macros in each successive column. Thus, some macros may be as long as 2^n primitive moves long, where n is the number of elements permuted. In the case of the 3x3x3 Rubik's Cube, macros can be as long as 2^{17} primitive moves.

While various group identities could be applied to reduce the lengths of the macros, the application of these identities is heuristic in nature and hence is not guaranteed to yield optimal macros. Following a different approach, Driscoll and Furst [Driscoll 83] have shown that for permutation groups whose generators are composed of cycles of bounded degree, solution lengths are $O(n^2)$. However, their algorithm would also generate inefficient solutions, relative to human strategies, due to the large constant factors involved.[2]

---

[2]personal communication with James Driscoll.

3.7 Conclusion

In conclusion, we find that many of the main ideas in this work can be found in one form or another in the literature of problem solving. The basic structure of the problem solver comes from GPS, the idea of learning by discovering parameters to a problem solving method was developed by Ernst and Goldstein, the study of non-serializable subgoals was pioneered in the blocks-world, the use of macro-operators dates from STRIPS, Banerji independently discovered the application of macros to non-serializable subgoals, and the structure of macro tables is borrowed from work on permutation groups. The novel contributions of this research are the combination of these ideas into a fairly general problem solving and learning method, and a precise theory of the applicability and performance of the technique.

4 The Macro Problem Solver

This chapter describes the operation of the Macro Problem Solver and gives several examples of its use. Briefly, the problem solver achieves an ordered set of subgoals one at a time by applying macros that solve the next subgoal while leaving previously solved subgoals intact, even though they may be temporarily violated during the application of the macro. We describe a problem representation, the structure of the table of macros, and the problem solving algorithm. The issue of how the macros are learned will be deferred to the following chapter. The collection of examples includes the Eight and Fifteen Puzzles, Rubik's Cube, the Think-A-Dot problem, and the Towers of Hanoi problem. For simplicity of exposition, the Eight Puzzle will be used as the primary example.

The Eight Puzzle (see Figure 4-1) has been studied extensively in the artificial intelligence literature [Schofield 67, Gaschnig 79, Ericsson 76] and provides one of the simplest examples of the operation of the Macro Problem Solver. It consists of a three by three frame which contains eight numbered square tiles. One of the squares of the frame is empty; this is referred to as the blank tile or blank. Any of the tiles horizontally or vertically adjacent to the blank can be moved into the blank position. The problem is to take an arbitrary initial configuration of the tiles and to transform it into a goal state, such as that shown in the figure, by sliding the tiles one at a time.

Figure 4-1: Eight Puzzle goal state

4.1 The State-Vector Representation

We begin with an abstract representation of our example problems. A state of a problem is specified by the values of a vector of state variables. Banerji [Banerji 83] argues that this representation is natural and very general. For example, the state variables for the Eight Puzzle are the nine different tiles of the puzzle, including the blank, and the values are the positions occupied by each tile in a particular state. For Rubik's Cube, the variables are the different cubies, and the values encode both the positions of the cubies and their orientation. In the case of the Towers of Hanoi, the variables are the disks, and the values are the pegs that the disks are on. For each problem, a single goal state is specified by assigning particular values to the state variables, called their goal values.

Note that a dual representation exists for these problems, and may in fact seem more intuitive to the reader. For example, in the Eight Puzzle the variables could correspond to the positions and the values could represent the tiles which occupy the positions. The two representations are equivalent, but we will deal with the former. The reason is that the macro problem solving technique is sensitive to the representation of the problem and in general will not work in the dual representation, as will be discussed in Chapter 6.

4.2 The Macro Table

Table 4-1 shows a *macro table* for the Eight Puzzle, corresponding to the goal state in Figure 4-1. The columns correspond to the tiles and the rows correspond to the tile positions. The labels of the positions coincide with the numbers of the tiles that occupy them in the goal state. The elements of the table are macros, which are sequences of primitive moves. A primitive move is represented by the first letter of Right, Left, Up, or Down, and is the direction that a tile is moved. This notation is unambiguous since only one tile, excluding the blank, can be moved in each direction from any given state.

The differences or subgoals used to solve the problem are the obvious ones of placing the tiles in their correct positions one at a time, or in other words, mapping the state variables to their goal values sequentially. The first thing that must be

Table 4-1: Macro table for the Eight Puzzle

TILES

POSITION	0	1	2	3	4	5	6
0							
1	UL						
2	U	RDLU					
3	UR	DLURRDLU	DLUR				
4	R	LDRURDLU	LDRU	RDLLURDRUL			
5	DR	ULDRURDLDRUL	LURDLDRU	LDRULURDDLUR	LURD		
6	D	URDLDRUL	ULDDRU	URDDLULDRRUL	ULDR	RDLLUURDLDRRUL	
7	DL	RULDDRUL	DRUULDRDLU	RULDRDLULDRRUL	URDLULDR	ULDRURDLLURD	URDL
8	L	DRUL	RULLDDRU	RDLULDRRUL	RULLDR	ULDRRULDLURD	RULD

```
The total number of non-identity macros is 35.
The average case solution length is 39.78 moves.
```

decided is the *solution order*, or the order in which the tiles are to be positioned. The constraints on solution orders will be discussed in detail in Chapter 6, and algorithms for selecting solution orders will be considered in Chapter 8. Roughly, the constraint is that the applicability and the effect of any operator on any state variable must be a function only of that state variable and previous state variables in the solution order. The only constraint on the solution order for the Eight Puzzle is that the blank be positioned first.

The columns of the table correspond to the state variables of the problem, which are the different tiles of the puzzle, in solution order from left to right. Each column contains the macros necessary to map its corresponding state variable to its goal value, without disturbing the values of the state variables that precede it in the solution order. The rows of the macro table correspond to the different possible values of the state variables, in our case the different possible positions of the tiles. For each tile and for each different position of the tile, there is a different macro that will move it to its goal position while leaving all the previously positioned tiles in their goal positions, independently of the positions of the remaining tiles in the solution order. More exactly, if the first $i-1$ state variables equal their respective goal values, then the macro in column i and row j of the macro table will map the value of the ith state variable in the solution order from the value corresponding to row j to its goal value, while leaving invariant the values of the first $i-1$ state variables in the solution order. For example, the macro in column 3 and row 6, **URDDLULDRRUL**, when applied to a state in which the blank and tiles 1 and 2 are in their goal positions, will map the 3 (or any other) tile to the goal position for the 3 tile, while leaving the blank, 1, and 2 tiles in their goal positions.

Note that in each column, one of the rows corresponds to the goal value of the corresponding state variable. Since nothing needs to be done to a state variable that already equals its goal value, we adopt the convention that these elements of the table contain the identity macro, which has zero length and no effect on the state of the problem. Notice also that the macro table for the Eight Puzzle has a lower triangular form. This is due to the fact that for this problem, no two state variables may have the same value, or in other words, no two tiles can occupy the same position. Thus, as more of the tiles are placed in their goal positions, there are fewer positions that the remaining tiles can occupy. Finally, note that the Eight Puzzle macro table ends with the 6 tile instead of the 8 tile. This is because once the first six tiles are in their goal positions, the remaining two tiles must also be correctly positioned, or the problem cannot be solved.

4.3 The Problem Solving Algorithm

The algorithm employed by the Macro Problem Solver will be described with the aid of the example in Figure 4-2. State a is an arbitrary initial state for the problem. The first step in the solution is to ascertain the position of the blank, which is located in the 5 position in state a. This value is used as a row index into the 0 column of the macro table and the corresponding macro, **DR**, is applied. The effect of the macro is to move the blank to the center position, its goal location. Next, the location of the 1 tile in state b is ascertained, position 2 in our example, this value is used as a row index into column 1 of the macro table, and the corresponding macro is applied. The effect of this macro is to move the 1 tile to its goal position, while

32

leaving the blank at its goal position. Note that *during* the application of the second macro the blank is moved, but by the *end* of the macro application, the blank is restored to the center position. Similarly, the position of the 2 tile in state *c* is used to select a macro from column 2 that will map the 2 tile to its goal position while leaving the blank and 1 tiles in their goal positions. Note that in state *d*, the 3 tile happens to be in its goal position already and hence the identity macro is applied, as is the case for tile 4 in state *e*. In general, for *i* from 1 to *n*, if *j* is the value of variable *i* in the solution order, apply the macro in column *i* and row *j*, and then repeat the process for the remaining variables. Note that the value of variable *i* above refers to its value at the *i*th stage of the solution process, and not to its value in the initial state.

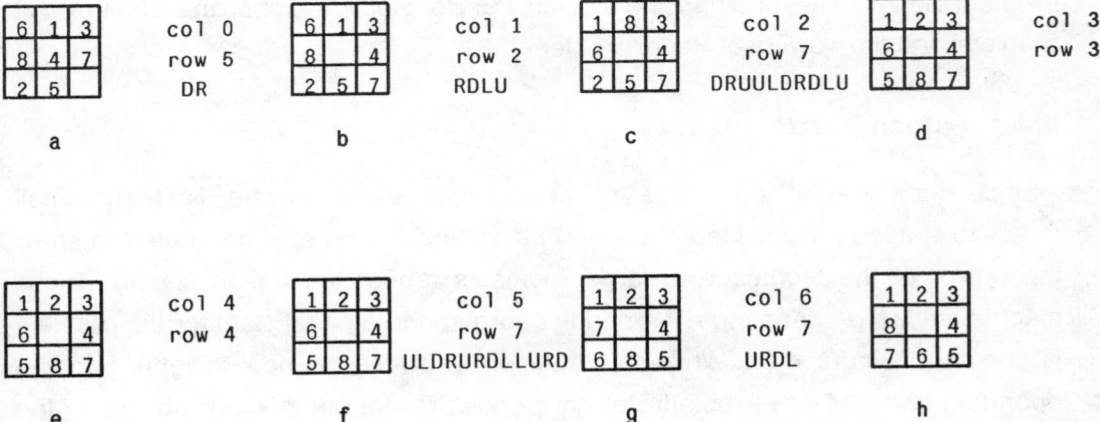

Figure 4-2: Example of solution of Eight Puzzle by the Macro Problem Solver

This solution algorithm will map any solvable initial state to the given goal state. The algorithm is deterministic, i.e. it involves no search, and hence is very efficient, running in time proportional to the number of primitive operators that are applied in the solution. It derives its power from the knowledge about the problem that is contained in the macros.

Unfortunately, the actual macro table is dependent on the particular goal state that is chosen. The algorithm can be simply extended, however, to allow mapping from any initial state to any goal state. The idea is to first find a solution from the initial state to the goal state for which the macro table was generated, then find a solution from the desired goal state to the goal state of the macro table, and finally compose the first solution with the inverse of the second solution. The inverse of a sequence of primitive operators is obtained by replacing each operator with its inverse and reversing the order of the operators. Hence, if each of our primitive operators has a primitive inverse, we can use the Macro Problem Solver to map from any initial state to any goal state with a penalty of approximately doubling the solution length.

4.4 Additional Examples

This section presents several additional examples of macro tables for the Macro Problem Solver. They include the Fifteen Puzzle, Rubik's Cube, the Think-A-Dot problem, and the Towers of Hanoi problem.

4.4.1 Fifteen Puzzle

Since the size of the state space for the Eight Puzzle is fairly small (181,440 states), a macro table for the Fifteen Puzzle was also generated to show the power of the technique in larger domains (about ten trillion states). These macros are listed in Appendix A1, and the corresponding goal state for the problem is shown in Figure 4-3. While this example provides no new insights into the operation of the Macro Problem Solver, it does present additional problems to the learning program as we will see in the following chapter.

1	2	3	4
5	6	7	8
9	10	11	12
13	14	15	

Figure 4-3: Fifteen Puzzle goal state

4.4.2 Rubik's Cube

For reasons already mentioned, Rubik's Cube was the primary vehicle for the development of the Macro Problem Solver. The state variables for this problem are the individual cubies, and the values encode both the positions and the orientations of the cubies. The subgoals are to position and orient the cubies correctly one at a time. Appendix A2 shows a macro table for the 2x2x2 cube.

Appendix A3 shows a macro table for the 3x3x3 Rubik's Cube. In addition to the eight corner cubies, there are twelve edge cubies, which have only two exposed facelets. The edge cubies are named by the planes of their two facelets in their goal positions. The complete set is {UL, UR, UF, UB, DL, DR, DF, DB, LF, LB, RF, RB}. An edge cubie can have two different orientations, labelled 0 and 1. The orientation of an edge cubie is the even-odd parity of the number of 90 degree rotations it has undergone, starting from the goal state. The moves of the 3x3x3 cube are represented identically to those of the 2x2x2 cube except that the Down, Left, and Back planes can be rotated as well.

4.4.3 Think-a-Dot

The Think-a-Dot problem is a commercially available toy which involves dropping marbles through gated channels and observing the effects on the gates. Figure 4-4 is a schematic diagram of the device. There are three input channels at the top, labelled A, B, and C, into which marbles can be dropped. When a marble is dropped in, it falls through a set of channels governed by eight numbered gates. Each gate has two states, Left and Right. When a marble encounters a gate, it goes left or right depending on the current state of the gate and then flips the gate to the opposite state. A state of the machine is specified by giving the states of each of the gates. The problem is to get from an arbitrary initial state to some goal state, such as all gates pointing Left.

This problem is included as an example for a number of reasons. First, it is a problem for which Goldstein's program was unable to find a good set of differences. For example, the subgoals of mapping one gate at a time to its goal value are not serializable. Secondly, it differs from the previous two examples in

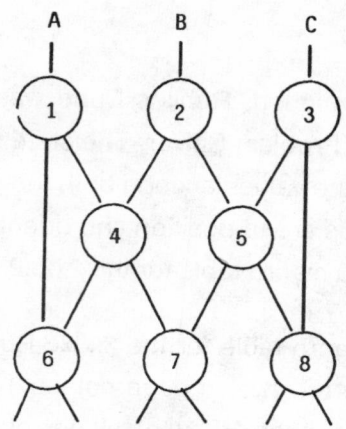

Figure 4-4: Think-a-Dot machine

that its states do not correspond to permutations of objects. Finally, the primitive operators of Think-a-Dot do not have inverses, even though if there exists a path from one state to another, then there always exists an inverse path. The reason is that given a primitive operator, there is no *single* (macro)operator which inverts the effect of the primitive operator on *every* state.

The state variables of the problem are the individual gates, and the values are Right and Left. The primitive operators are A, B, and C, corresponding to dropping a marble in each of the input gates. Table 4-2 shows a macro table for the Think-a-Dot problem where the goal state is all gates pointing Left. Note that there are only two possible values for each state variable and hence only two macros in each column, one of which is the identity macro. The last gate in the macro table is gate 7 since once the first seven gates are set, the state of the last gate is determined, due to a situation similar to that of the Eight Puzzle.

Table 4-2: Macro table for the Think-a-Dot machine

	GATES						
	1	2	3	4	5	6	7
Right	A	B	C	AA	CC	AAAA	CCCC
Left							

4.4.4 Towers of Hanoi

The well-known Towers of Hanoi problem (see Figure 4-5) consists of three pegs and a set of different size disks stacked on the pegs in decreasing order of size. The standard task is to transfer all the disks from one peg to another subject to the constraints that only one disk may be moved at a time and that a larger disk may never be placed on top of a smaller disk. Note that while the standard treatment of the problem is only concerned with solving the problem from a particular initial state, namely all the disks stacked on one peg, we will address the issue of transferring all the disks to a goal peg from any legal initial state. A legal state is one where no disk is on top of a smaller disk on the same peg.

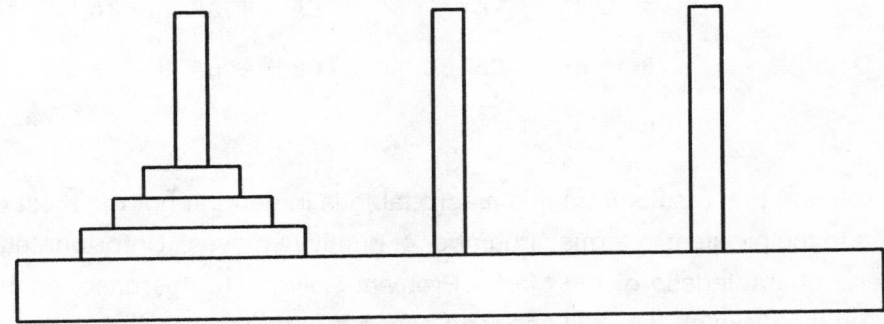

Figure 4-5: Towers of Hanoi problem

In contrast to the previous examples, this problem is easily solved by GPS, and Goldstein's program was able to find the correct differences. In fact, it is often viewed as the classic GPS problem, yet is included here for several reasons. One is that it demonstrates that the Macro Problem Solver is not restricted to problems that GPS cannot handle but rather overlaps GPS in its coverage of problems. Another reason is that the Towers of Hanoi is such a well-known problem in artificial intelligence that its treatment by the Macro Problem Solver allows comparison of our method with other problem solving paradigms.

Table 4-3 shows a macro table for the three-disk Towers of Hanoi problem, where the goal peg is peg C. A similar table can be built for any number of disks. The state variables are the disks, numbered 1 through 3 in increasing order of size. The values are the different pegs the disks could be on, namely A, B, and C. There are six primitive moves in the problem space, one corresponding to each possible ordered pair of source peg and destination peg. Since only the top disk on a peg can be moved, this is an unambiguous representation of the operators. The complete set is thus {AB, AC, BA, BC, CA, CB}. The solution order is to position the disks in increasing order of size. Note that this is exactly the opposite of the ordering of subgoals for the GPS solution to the problem, but does correspond to the order in which the disks are first moved in the GPS solution.

Table 4-3: Macro table for the three disk Towers of Hanoi problem

		DISKS	
	1	2	3
P A	AC	CB AC BC	CA CB AB AC BA BC AC
E			
G B	BC	CA BC AC	CB CA BA BC AB AC BC
S			
C			

The solution that results from this macro table is in general not the most efficient solution to the problem in terms of number of primitive moves. Unfortunately, this is a general characteristic of the Macro Problem Solver. In this case, each macro stacks up the disks on the goal peg, and hence the next macro must move them to create a larger stack on the goal peg. In Chapter 8 we will discuss the issue of more efficient macro tables for this problem.

4.5 Conclusions

The knowledge necessary to efficiently solve a certain class of problems can be represented by macro-operator sequences. The key property of these macros is that they leave all previously satisfied subgoals invariant while solving an additional subgoal as well. The macros can be organized into a two-dimensional macro table such that a problem solving program can solve any instance of the problem with no search. The result is an expert problem solving system for a given problem.

The method has been illustrated by a number of example problems, including the Eight and Fifteen Puzzles, the 2x2x2 and 3x3x3 Rubik's Cubes, the Think-a-Dot problem, and the Towers of Hanoi problem. These problems were chosen for their diversity and each one in fact represents an entire class of problems for which the Macro Problem Solver is equally effective. For example, Rubik's Cubes are only two of a large class of puzzles that involve twisting various geometric solids, sliding tile puzzles may have arbitrary geometries including one where cubes with orientation are rolled into the blank position, the Towers of Hanoi Problem becomes even more interesting with a larger number of pegs, and the Think-a-Dot problem can be generalized to any directed acyclic graph.

5 Learning Macro-Operators

While the previous chapter described the operation of the Macro Problem Solver once it has a complete macro table, this chapter is concerned with the problem of how the macros are acquired. This is the learning component of the paradigm. The basic technique that will be used is to search the space of macro-operators. Each macro generated is inserted into the macro table in its correct slot, unless a shorter macro already occupies that slot. We first address the problem of where to place a given macro in the macro table. We then consider three different methods for generating macros. One is a simple brute-force search through the space of primitive operator sequences. The second is a variation of bi-directional search. The last is the macro composition technique of Sims [Sims 70]. In addition, some techniques for the efficient use of memory are described to enable the search to proceed as far as possible. Finally, the design of a problem-independent macro learning program is presented by separating the problem-dependent components from the domain-independent ones.

5.1 Assigning Macros to the Macro Table

In general, the macros that make up the macro table all have the property that they leave an initial sequence of the state variables invariant if they equal their goal values, and map the next state variable to its goal value, independent of the values of the remaining variables in the solution order. In addition, the table should be filled with the shortest macros that accomplish each subgoal. This section is concerned with the problem of determining the correct location in the macro table of a given macro.

5.1.1 Selecting the Column

In order to determine the column in the macro table in which an arbitrary macro belongs, we introduce the notion of the *invariance* of a macro. Given a particular goal state, a solution order, and a macro-operator, we define the invariance of the macro as follows: The macro is applied to the goal state of the problem and the resulting state is compared with the goal state. The invariance of the macro is the number of consecutive state variables of the resulting state that equal their corresponding goal values. The sequence starts with the first state variable in the solution order and continues until a mismatch is found. In other words, if the first state variable of the resulting state does not equal its goal value, the invariance of the macro is zero; if the first variable in the solution order equals its goal value but the second does not, the invariance of the macro is one; and in general if the first i state variables in the solution order equal their goal values but the $i + 1^{st}$ does not, then the invariance of the macro is i. For example, if the goal state of the Eight Puzzle is represented by the vector [B 1 2 3 4 5 6 7 8], the solution order is (B 1 2 3 4 5 6 7 8), and the state resulting from the application of some particular macro to the goal state is [B 1 2 3 6 5 7 4 8], then the invariance of the macro is four, because the first four tiles (including the blank) in the solution order are in their goal positions and the fifth is not.

The invariance of a macro gives the longest initial subsequence of state variables in the solution order that are left invariant by the application of the macro to the goal state. Hence, the invariance of a macro determines its column in the macro table.

5.1.2 Selecting the Row

In addition to the column, we must also determine the proper row for a macro in order to include it in the macro table. A macro in column i and row j of the macro table, when applied to a state in which the first i variables in the solution order have their goal values and in which the $i + 1^{st}$ variable has the value corresponding to row j, results in a state in which the first $i + 1$ variables have their goal values. Hence, the row in the table of a macro with invariance i is the row that corresponds to the value of the $i + 1^{st}$ state variable that the macro maps to the goal value.

In general, determining the row of a macro requires computing the inverse of the macro. For some problems, however, including Think-a-Dot, Rubik's Cube, and the Eight Puzzle, the row of a macro can be determined directly from the macro itself. We will first describe the general technique, and then show how the row can be obtained without inverses.

First, note that if a macro has invariance i, then its inverse will also have invariance i, where the inverse is obtained by reversing the order of the operators and replacing each with its inverse operator. The reason is that the original macro maps the first i variables from their goal values back to their goal values and hence the inverse must do the same. Second, if the $i + 1^{st}$ state variable has the value corresponding to row j after the application of the inverse macro to the goal state, then the correct row of the original macro in the macro table is j. The reason is that the inverse macro maps the value of the $i + 1^{st}$ variable from its goal value to that corresponding to j, and hence the original macro would map the value corresponding to j back to the goal value. Thus, given a macro with invariance i, we place it in the table at column i, and at the row which corresponds to the value of the $i + 1^{st}$ variable in the solution order when the inverse macro is applied to the goal state.

With the Towers of Hanoi problem, however, there is no guarantee that a macro that is applicable to the goal state will necessarily be useful from any other states. For example, if the goal peg is peg **C**, then the single operator **CA** does not belong in the macro table at all because it doesn't move any disk to the goal peg. In that case, the inverse macro, which does move a disk to the goal peg, is inserted in the macro table.

We now turn our attention to the direct method of determining the row of a macro without computing the inverse macro. For example, in the Eight Puzzle, the row of a macro with invariance i can be determined by applying the macro to the goal state, and then finding the tile that is mapped to the $i + 1$ position, or in other words, the state variable with value $i + 1$. For Rubik's Cube, the row of a macro with invariance i is found by applying the macro to the goal state, and then finding the cubie that is mapped to the $i + 1^{st}$ cubicle. However, this only gives the position component of the row value. The orientation component is obtained by taking the inverse of the orientation of the same cubie. In other words, we combine the cubie in the $i + 1^{st}$ position with the inverse of its orientation. The two possible orientations of edge cubies are inverses of each other, while for the corner cubies the original orientation is its own inverse and clockwise and counterclockwise orientations are inverses of each other. In the case of the Think-A-Dot problem, the row simply corresponds to the value of the next variable in the solution order after the invariant component. Since there are only two values, this is just the first non-goal value. If the macro changed it from goal to non-goal, then applying it again will flip it back to the goal value.

5.2 Brute-Force Search

Given the above techniques for placing a macro in its correct place in the macro table, what is still required for the learning program is a method of generating macros. Since we are interested in the shortest possible macros for each slot in the table, we first adopt a brute-force, depth-first iterative deepening search. Depth-first iterative deepening is a search algorithm which first expands the first level of the search tree, then performs a depth-first search to level two, followed by a depth-first search to level three, etc. It uses far less memory than breadth-first search, yet always finds a shortest path to the goal. Thus, the first macro placed in each empty slot in the table is guaranteed to be a minimal length macro for that slot.

It is important to realize that a single search from the goal state will find all the macros in the table, and that a separate search for each column or even each entry is not required. We are not searching for particular states but rather for particular operator sequences. For problems like Rubik's Cube that have no preconditions on the operators, a single search will encounter all possible operator sequences up to the length of the search depth, and hence will find all macros up to that length. For problems with operator preconditions, such as the Towers of Hanoi, recall that we are only interested in macros that map some initial subsequence of the state variables in the solution order to their goal values. Hence, by searching from the complete goal state and using the inverses of the operator sequences generated, we will find all the macros in a single search.

One problem with this learning algorithm is knowing when to terminate it. We cannot simply run it until all the slots in the macro table are filled because some slots may remain permanently empty. For example, the last two columns of the Eight Puzzle macro table can never be filled, due to the property of the puzzle that only even permutations of the tiles can be reached from a given state, and hence the positions of the last two tiles are determined once the positions of the remaining tiles are known. Both Rubik's Cube and the Think-A-Dot problems have similar properties. In general, discovering these properties is very difficult. Hence, we have a situation of not knowing when we know enough to solve every instance of the problem.

There are several solutions to this difficulty. One is simply to run the learning program until its computational resources, in most cases memory, are exhausted. Another is the heuristic of terminating the search if one or two additional plies fail to produce any new macros. The best solution[1] involves interleaving the learning program with the problem solving program as co-routines and only running the learning program when a new macro is needed to solve some particular problem instance.

Brute-force, depth-first iterative deepening is sufficient to solve the Eight Puzzle, the Towers of Hanoi, and the Think-A-Dot problems. For problems as large as the Fifteen Puzzle and the Rubik's Cubes, however, a more sophisticated technique is required.

5.3 Partial-Match, Bi-Directional Search

If we assume that each primitive operator has an inverse primitive operator, thus ruling out the Think-A-Dot example, then we can find macros considerably more efficiently than by depth-first iterative deepening. Consider a macro that leaves i state variables invariant. When applied to the goal state, the values of these state variables are mapped from their goal values, through a succession of intermediate values, and finally back to their goal values again. Now consider splitting in half the sequence of primitive operators that make up the macro. The first half maps the i state variables from their goal values to a sequence of values $(v_1, v_2, \ldots, v_i)$, and the

---

[1] suggested by Jon Bentley

45

second half maps these values back to their goal values. Thus, the inverse of the second half of the macro will map the goal values of these variables to this same set of values $(v_1, v_2, \ldots, v_i)$. This suggests that, given two different macros that map the same initial subsequence of i state variables, according to the solution order, from their goal values to an identical set of intermediate values, composing one of the macros with the inverse of the other will yield a macro with invariance i. Thus, macros can be found by storing the intermediate values of the state variables for each macro when applied to the goal state and comparing them with the corresponding values for each new macro generated, looking for matches among initial subsequences of variables according to the solution order.

Note that once a match is found, two macros can be generated, depending on which of the two matching submacros is inverted. The two macros are inverses of each other. Hence, each of these macros must have the same invariance, but in general the rows of the macro table to which they belong may be different. Furthermore, by using the inverse method for determining the row of a macro, the correct row for each of the macros can easily be determined from the other. Note that this is not a heuristic method but is in fact guaranteed to find all minimal length macros, since every macro can be split into two parts as described.

This scheme is closely related to bi-directional search, first analyzed by Pohl [Pohl 71]. They have in common searching for a path from both ends simultaneously, looking for a match between states generated from opposite directions, and then composing the path from one direction with the inverse of the path from the other direction. There are, however, three important differences between this technique and bi-directional search. One is that in this case the initial and goal states are the same state, namely the goal state, and hence only one search is necessary instead of two. The second difference is that, since we are looking for macros that leave only some subset of the state variables invariant, we only require a partial match of the state variables rather than a total match. Finally, in order to save space and find the shortest macros, the bi-directional search is combined with depth-first iterative deepening.

The computational advantage of this scheme is tremendous. In order to find a macro of length d, instead of searching to depth d, we need only search to depth

$\lceil d/2 \rceil$. Since the computation time for a complete depth-first search is proportional to b^d, where b is the branching factor and d is the depth of the search, this reduces the computation time from b^d to $b^{d/2}$, essentially halving the exponent, assuming the matching can be done efficiently.

If each new state must be individually compared to each existing state, a bi-directional search requires as much time as a uni-directional search, with most of the time taken up doing the comparisons. Thus, the performance claimed above can only be achieved if a new state can be compared to all the existing states in constant time.

Fortunately, hashing the states based on the values of the state variables will achieve this performance. To find a macro with invariance i, a match among the first i state variables must be made, which implies that the hash function may not depend on any other state variables. The reason is that including another variable in the hash function in which the two states do not match may result in their being mapped to different parts of the hash table. This presents a problem in that, while searching for macros with low invariance, there is very little information that can be used by a hash function to separate the states in the table. On the other hand, when searching for macros with greater invariance, an effective hash function is essential for tolerable performance of the search algorithm.

In order to resolve this difficulty, we make use of the fact that macros with low invariance are relatively common while macros with high invariance are much rarer. Thus, in an iterative deepening bi-directional search, the macros to fill the low invariance columns of the macro table will be found fairly early, and subsequent effort can be focused on macros with greater invariance, allowing a more effective hashing function to be used. The search algorithm works by maintaining an *invariance threshold*, which at any given point in the search is the minimum invariance for which all the elements in the corresponding column of the macro table have not yet been filled. At the end of each iteration of the search, if the invariance threshold has increased, then the states in the next iteration are hashed using a more discriminating hash function constructed by incorporating the additional state variable(s) corresponding to the columns that were filled since the last iteration, and the search continues. This allows the low invariance macros to be found and also permits an effective hash function to be used for searching for the high invariance macros, which occupies most of the search.

An alternative scheme for comparing the generated states efficiently uses a search tree instead of a hash table. As each state is generated, it is stored in a tree where each level of the tree corresponds to a different state variable and different nodes at the same level correspond to different possible values for that state variable. The ordering of levels of the tree from top to bottom corresponds to the solution order of the state variables from first to last. Thus, each node of the tree corresponds to an assignment of values to an initial subsequence of state variables in the solution order.

A state is inserted in the tree by filtering it down from the root node to the last existing node which corresponds to a previously generated state. A new node is created at the next level of the tree and the macro which generated the new state is stored at the new node. Since the states are generated using iterative deepening, this ensures that with each existing node is stored a shortest macro which maps the goal state to the initial subsequence of values corresponding to the node. When a new state reaches the last previously existing node it matches in the tree, a macro is created as before.

The expected number of probes to compare a new state to the existing states for the hashing scheme is constant, assuming the hash table remains partly empty [Knuth 73]. For the search tree, the expected number of comparisons is linear in the number of state variables. The partial-match, iterative deepening bi-directional search algorithm is sufficient to find all the macros for the Fifteen Puzzle and the 2x2x2 Rubik's Cube. The limitation of this algorithm, as for any bi-directional search, is the amount of memory available for storing states.

5.4 Macro Composition

Finding all the macros up to length nine for the 3x3x3 Rubik's Cube macro table requires about 100,000 words of memory. This still leaves seven empty slots, out of 238, in the table. These remaining slots can be filled using the macro composition technique employed by Sims [Sims 70].

48

If we compose two macros with invariance i, the result will also be a macro with invariance at least i, but in general a different macro. If, in addition, when the macros are applied to the goal state the two $i + 1^{st}$ variables take on the same values, but not necessarily the goal values, then if we compose either macro with the inverse of the other macro, the result will be a macro with invariance at least $i + 1$. This is actually just a special case of the more general technique described in the previous section, specialized in the sense that not only are the first i variables constrained to match, but they must equal the goal values as well.

The advantage of this technique is that it allows us to find macros with high invariance with very little computation, by using macros with high invariance that have already been found. The disadvantage of the technique is that a macro found by this method will not in general be the shortest macro for the corresponding slot in the macro table. In fact, there is some psychological plausibility to this method for finding macros in that many human cube solvers, particularly novices, use compositions of shorter macros to complete the final stages in their solution strategies.

The macro composition technique is effective in finding the remaining seven macros for Rubik's Cube that are beyond the range of the bi-directional search. Most of these macros are fourteen moves long whereas macros twelve moves long exist for these slots in the table. The complete learning program for the 3x3x3 Rubik's Cube runs for less than 15 minutes of CPU time on a VAX/11-780 and uses about 200K words of memory.

Note that macro composition could be used to find all the macros for Rubik's Cube, starting with only the primitive operators of the problem. However, as pointed out in section 3.6, the resulting strategy would be extremely inefficient in terms of number of primitive moves. The combination of bi-directional search and macro composition amounts to a tradeoff between learning time and space vs. solution efficiency. An alternative approach to the computational limitations of bi-directional search, that of decomposing the problem, will be presented in section 8.2.3.

5.5 Efficient Use of Memory

Since the amount of available memory is what limits the search for macros, memory must be used as efficiently as possible. In particular, we would like to minimize the amount of memory required for each entry in the hash table. There are two pieces of information to be stored with each hash table entry: a description of the state, in order to match the state variables, and the macro which led to the state, in order to construct the macros that result from a match. In the following discussion, we assume that our memory is divided into words of w bits. Typical values for w are 32 and 36 bits.

In general, the macro component of a hash table entry can be encoded in a single word. The intuitive reason for this is that the number of different macros we will be able to store will be far less than 2^w. If we represent our primitive operators by the integers zero through k inclusive, then a sequence of primitive operators can be packed into a word, without loss of information, by storing the equivalent integer in base $k + 1$. For example, a Think-a-Dot macro such as [A B C A] would be encoded in the integer $0 \cdot 3^3 + 1 \cdot 3^2 + 2 \cdot 3^1 + 1 \cdot 3^0 = 16_{10}$.

In order to pack every macro into a single word, we must be careful to encode the primitive operators so that the number of operators is close to the effective branching factor of the space. Otherwise, if preconditions and redundant operations eliminate most operator sequences, then we may be able to search to the depth of longer macros than can be encoded in a single word. For example, if the primitive operators of the Eight Puzzle are represented by ordered pairs of source and destination positions, we get 24 different operators. However, we can unambiguously represent the primitive operators by giving the direction a tile is to be moved: left, right, up, or down. This is still somewhat redundant since the average branching factor of the space is only 1.67 (see section 7.3).

How much memory is required for the state description component of a hash table entry? If there are s distinct states in the space, then the number of words required to encode a state is $(\log s)/w$. The macro together with the goal state, however, completely determine the resulting state. Hence, there is no need to store the state in the hash table at all. Instead, each time a new state must be compared with the existing hash table entry, the existing state can be regenerated by unpacking the macro and applying it to the goal state.

While the above argument shows that in principle we only need one word of memory per hash table entry, in practice the constant regeneration of states requires a great deal of computation time. A more time-efficient strategy, at the expense of doubling the space requirement, is to use an additional word per hash table entry to represent as much of the state as can be encoded in a single word. As in the case of a macro, if v is the number of different possible values for a state variable, then the values of $w/\log v$ state variables can be stored in a single word as an integer base v. Only if a new state matches an existing entry in these state variables, as well as hashing to the same value, does the entire state have to be regenerated from the macro.

Since much of the information about the values of the state variables used in the hash function is reflected in the location of an entry in the hash table, the variables stored in the additional word should be chosen to be different from those used in the hash function Both these sets of state variables must be chosen from the first t state variables in the solution order, where t is the current invariance threshold of the macro search.

5.6 Design of a Problem-Independent Macro Learning Program

In this section we sketch a design for a macro learning program that is independent of any particular problem domain. This is accomplished by separating the components of the learning program into those that depend on the problem domain and those that are problem-independent, while striving to minimize the problem-dependent components of the system. First the problem-dependent components will be presented followed by the problem-independent ones. We assume throughout that a state is represented by the values of a vector of state variables and that each primitive operator has an inverse primitive operator.

5.6.1 Problem-Dependent Components

Perhaps the most obvious problem-dependent component is the actual goal state itself. Recall that the entire macro table is dependent on the selection of a particular goal state. In addition, a computer model of the problem must be provided, most conveniently in the form of an operator application function and a legal move generator. The operator application function takes a state and a primitive operator as arguments and returns the state that results from applying the primitive operator to the given state. The legal move generator takes a current state and the last operator that was applied to reach that state as arguments and returns the set of primitive operators that generate new states, taking into account any preconditions on the operators. While the last operator applied is not strictly necessary as an argument to this function, it allows the legal move generator to exclude redundant moves such as the inverse of the last operator.

Another important problem-dependent component of the macro learning program is the solution order, or the sequence in which the state variables are to be mapped to their goal values. The constraints on the solution order will be considered in Chapter 6, and heuristics for choosing a solution order that results in efficient solutions will be discussed in Chapter 8.

In order to pack macros into a word efficiently, the total number of primitive operators must be known. In addition, in order to construct a macro once a match between state variables is found, the inverses of each of the primitive operators must be provided. Furthermore, the dimensions of the macro table are determined by the number of state variables and the number of different values they can assume.

A subtle but important piece of problem-dependent information is some means of determining the number of slots in each column of the macro table which remain empty in the complete table. This is necessary in order to allow the invariance threshold to increase to take advantage of more effective hashing functions as the search progresses. For example, in a problem like the Eight Puzzle where the states are permutations of a set of values, the learning program must know that if variable i has value j for its goal value, then row j of the macro table will be empty for all columns greater than i in the solution order. Otherwise, the invariance threshold will never advance beyond the second column of the macro table due to the empty slot, and the remainder of the search will be crippled by a hash function based on only the first two state variables. In addition, such information is useful for terminating the learning program when the macro table is completely filled.

5.6.2 Problem-Independent Components

The remaining components of the macro learning program are problem-independent. We briefly discuss the major modules below.

First, a number of utility functions are required. These include functions that pack and unpack macros, mapping between sequences of primitive operators and their integer encodings. In addition, there must be a macro application function that takes a macro and a state as arguments and returns the state that results from the application of the macro to the given state. This function is problem-independent, but relies very heavily on the problem-dependent operator application function.

The hashing function is of critical importance to the performance of the learning program. As mentioned earlier, the hash function is different for different levels of the search. Recall that the number of state variables that can be encoded in a word is $h = w/\log v$, where v is the number of different state variable values. If the invariance threshold t is less than or equal to h, then the first t state variables in the solution order are used in the hash function. Once the invariance threshold exceeds h, then h state variables are chosen for the hash function, uniformly distributed from among the first t variables in the order.

The search function generates one ply of the search space per call and passes each state generated one at a time to a state processing function. This function hashes the state and scans the hash table for a state whose state descriptor word matches the given state, passing both states to a comparison function for each match it finds. The comparison function regenerates the stored state and calls a macro processing function if the match between the two states is greater than the invariance threshold. This function generates the complete macro and its inverse, places them in their correct slots in the macro table if those slots are empty, marks the slots full, and increases the invariance threshold if an entire column is filled as a result. Finally, there is a main program that, in addition to other initialization functions, places the primitive operators, or macros of length one, in their respective slots in the macro table.

5.7 Conclusions

We have presented a number of techniques for learning macros effectively. These include depth-first iterative deepening search, a variation of bi-directional search that is only single-ended and requires only a partial match of the states, and the macro composition technique of Sims. Since the performance of the learning program is limited by the amount of available memory for a hash table, it is shown that an entry in the table requires only one word of memory. Finally, a design for a problem-independent macro learning program is presented by separating the problem-dependent components from the problem-independent ones. The most important results of this chapter are that all the macros in the table can be found in a single search from the goal state and that filling the macro table is feasible for problems of substantial size (e.g. the 3x3x3 Rubik's Cube).

6 The Theory of Macro Problem Solving

We have seen that macro problem solving works for a set of example problems, and have demonstrated the learning of macro-operators. We now turn our attention to the question of why these techniques work. The reason for addressing this issue is twofold: to understand the problem structure it is based on, and to characterize the range of problems for which it is effective. The main contribution of this chapter is to identify a property of problem spaces called *operator decomposability*. Roughly, operator decomposability exists in a problem space to the extent that the effect of an operator on a state can be decomposed into its effect on each individual component of the state, independently of the other components of the state. It will be shown that operator decomposability is a sufficient condition for the application of macro problem solving. In addition, the technique will be generalized to admit arbitrary intermediate states.

The theory of macro problem solving will be presented in two parts. We will first address the special case in which states are described by a vector of state variables and the subgoals are to achieve the goal values of state variables. We will then consider the more general theory which admits any type of state description and arbitrary subgoals. The theory will be presented in the order in which it was discovered. The rationale for this is that the path of discovery is interesting in itself and is also most likely to be the "path of least resistance" for the reader.

Given the representation of a problem as a vector of state variables, the behavior of the Macro Problem Solver can be described as follows. The order of columns in the macro table implies an ordering of the state variables. The macros in the first column are used to map the first state variable from whatever value it has in the initial state to its goal value. The macros of the second column map the second variable to its goal value and leave the first variable equal to its goal value. Similarly, each of the other columns of macros are used to map the values of their corresponding state variables to their goal values from whatever values they have at that stage of the solution process, while leaving all the previous variables equal to their goal values.

6.1 What is the Value of Non-Serializable Subgoals?

If we view the values of the state variables between macro applications, the values of an initial subsequence of variables in the solution order will equal their goal values. At each stage of the solution, the length of this sequence increases by one. However, if we observe these values in the middle of a macro application, there is no guarantee that any of the variables will equal their goal values. If we observe an entire solution sequence ignoring the boundaries between macros, then after a variable achieves its goal value, in general its value will later change to a new value, and this will happen a number of times before the final goal state is reached. Since a state variable does not remain at its goal value once it is achieved, what is the purpose of achieving the goal value the first time and each time thereafter except for the last?[1]

The relevance of the question becomes clear when we compare it with the corresponding question for the situation where we have serializable subgoals. In that case, the goal state is a conjunction of subgoals and solving a particular subgoal represents progress toward the goal in the sense that the number of remaining subgoals to be satisfied decreases. However, we cannot make the same claim if a subgoal is to be violated after it is achieved.

Even if it is subsequently violated, achieving a non-serializable subgoal may represent progress because it moves us closer to the goal by the metric of minimum number of moves in the problem space, which is often the case. However, the experiments reported in Chapter 2 show that at least for the 2x2x2 Rubik's Cube, the minimum number of moves to the goal state is independent of the number of solved subgoals. Yet, the 2x2x2 cube is one of the examples for which the Macro Problem Solver works. Hence, the question of the utility of these subgoals remains to be answered.

---

[1]This question was raised by Allen Newell.

6.2 Macro Tables from Random Intermediate Goals

Since the particular subgoals we used to solve the 2x2x2 cube bear no relation to distance from the final goal, we might ask whether an arbitrary set of subgoals might do just as well. Surprisingly, the answer turns out to be yes!

Consider the macro table for solving the 2x2x2 Rubik's Cube shown in Appendix A4. Each set of macros corresponds to a set of partially specified intermediate states generated as follows: First, a random solution order was generated: (URF ULF ULB URB DLF DRF DRB). Then, for the first intermediate state, a random position and orientation (DLF, 1) was chosen for the first cubie (URF), from the set of legal values. For the second stage, random positions and orientations were chosen for both the first and second cubies. Similarly, random values are chosen for the remaining intermediate states. The final state is the actual goal state of the problem. The only constraint on this process is that each partially specified state ·must correspond to at least one legal state in the problem space. In particular, in this case each value must represent a different cubie from all the other values at that stage.

The first group of macros in the table map the first cubie (URF) to position DLF and orientation 1, which is not its goal value, from each possible value it could have in the initial state. The second group of macros map the second cubie (ULF) to (DRB, 1) which again is not its goal value. At the same time, these macros all map (URF) from (DLF, 1) to (DRF, 0). The macros in the remaining group behave similarly. Finally, the last group of macros in the table maps the last intermediate state to the goal state.

This table illustrates two important generalizations of the Macro Problem Solver. One is that the *target values* of variables in the intermediate states need not be their goal values. The second is that the target values of a particular variable need not be invariant over successive stages but may change from stage to stage. The only requirements are that at each stage, the values of all previous variables in the solution order must be known, and they must correspond to at least one legal state in the problem space.

There is a penalty in learning time for allowing the value of a variable to change from one intermediate state to another. For the "standard" macro table which uses goal values for the target values, the entire table can be filled in with one search starting from the goal state. If we allow target values to be different from the goal values, but still require them to remain constant from one intermediate state to the next, then we can still fill in the table with a single search starting from the state specified by the set of target values. The goal state is then reached by including a single macro at the end of the table which maps the target state to the goal state. However, if we allow the target values to change from one intermediate state to the next, then we will in general need a separate search for each column of the macro table, starting from the state specified by the target values at that point. On the other hand, since the running time of the learning program is dominated by the depth of the longest search, this does not increase the order of the running time.

What is the effect of allowing these extra degrees of freedom in the macro tables on the efficiency of the resulting solutions, in terms of number of primitive moves? In general, constructing a table from random intermediate states will result in a less efficient strategy, since random subgoals will not move the problem closer to solution. However, in the case of the 2x2x2 Rubik's Cube, the standard subgoals do not converge on the goal in terms of number of primitive moves. Hence, the strategy that corresponds to the macro table built using random intermediate states (Appendix A4), should be as efficient, in terms of number of primitive moves, as the strategy built from the standard intermediate states (Appendix A2). In fact, the average case solution length for the random intermediate states is 32.83 moves, while the standard subgoals result in an average case solution length of 27.00 moves. This discrepancy is due to the fact that with the standard subgoals, at each stage of the solution there is a small probability that the next subgoal will also be satisfied and hence no macro need be applied. However, with intermediate states which change from one stage to the next, a macro must be applied at each stage. This feature also shows up in the difference in the number of non-identity macros in the two tables (75 vs. 80).

On the other hand, by taking advantage of this extra freedom and cleverly selecting target values, slightly more efficient solutions than those resulting from

58

goal target values can be achieved for some problems, as will be shown in section 8.1.2.

Viewed in this light, the Macro Problem Solver appears to embody an extremely general method. We simply randomly generate a set of intermediate states, subject to the constraint that each of the partially specified intermediate states correspond to a legal state in the problem space, and then fill in the macro table. However, we haven't yet placed any constraints on the problem in order to apply the method.

If we restrict our set of subgoals to contain just the main goal, then the Macro Problem Solver in fact becomes a universal method which amounts to simply precomputing and storing the solution to every possible problem instance. However, the usefulness of the method depends on the number of macros required. The reason it is an effective technique for our examples is that a very small number of macros are required, relative to the size of the space. What properties of a problem allow a very efficient strategy for a very large number of problem instances to be expressed with a very small number of macros?

6.3 Operator Decomposability

When we examine the macro table for the 2x2x2 Rubik's Cube (Appendix A2), we notice that the first column contains 21 entries, including the identity macro. There is one macro for each possible combination of position and orientation that the first cubie in the solution order could occupy in the initial state, or one macro for each possible value of the first state variable. Thus, the choice of what macro to apply first depends only on the value of the first state variable. Another way of looking at this is that for a given value of the first variable, the same macro will map it to its target value regardless of the values of the remaining state variables.

In general, this property would not hold for an arbitrary problem. In fact, in the worst case, one would need a different macro in the first column for each different initial state of the problem. If we needed a different macro for each initial state for just the first stage of the solution, we may as well store the macro which gives the complete solution. As mentioned above, this reduces the method to nothing more than pre-computing the solution to all possible problem instances and storing the results.

Returning to our example, we notice that in the second column as well, we only need one macro for each possible value of the second state variable. Again, this is due to the fact that its application is independent of the values of all succeeding variables in the solution order. Note that the actual macros themselves are very much dependent on the value of the first state variable. However, this value is fixed by the pre-determined intermediate states. Similarly, for the remaining columns of the table, the macros depend only on the previous state variables in the solution order and are independent of the succeeding variables.

This property can be characterized by examining the definitions of the operators in terms of the state variables. For Rubik's Cube, each operator will affect some subset of the cubies or state variables, and leave the remaining state variables unchanged. However, the resulting position and orientation of each cubie as a result of any twist is solely a function of that cubie's position and orientation before the twist was applied, and independent of the positions and orientations of the other cubies. We refer to this property as *operator decomposability*.

The following sections will formalize this notion and show that operator decomposability is a sufficient condition for the existence of a non-trivial macro table. For simplicity, we restrict the theory to the case where the target values of the state variables are their goal values. It could easily be extended to encompass arbitrary target values.

6.3.1 General Definitions

We begin the formal treatment with precise definitions of what is meant by a problem, a problem instance, a macro, and a macro table. In general, capital letters will be used to denote sets, bold face will be used for vectors and vector functions, and normal face will be used for scalars and scalar functions.

Definition 1: We define a *problem* **P** to be a triple (**S**, **O**, g) where:

S is a set of states and each state $s \in S$ is a vector of state variables $(s_1, s_2, \ldots, s_n)$, where the s_i are chosen from a set of values $V = \{v_1, v_2, \ldots, v_h\}$. Note that in general $S \subset V^n$, where V^n is the set of all n-element vectors with elements chosen from V.

O is a set of operators where each operator $o \in O$ is a total function from **S** to **S**. We will write $o(s) = t$ to denote the application of operator **o** to state **s** resulting in state **t**. In the event that there are preconditions on the operators, then $\forall s \in S$ and $o \in O$ s.t. s does not satisfy the preconditions of operator **o**, we adopt the convention that $o(s) = s$.

$g \in S$ is a particular state called the *goal state*, represented by the vector $(g_1, g_2, \ldots, g_n)$, where each g_i is called the *goal value* of variable i.

Let S_i be the set of all states in which the first $i - 1$ state variables equal their goal values or

$$s \in S_i \text{ iff } s \in S \text{ and } \forall x, 1 \leq x \leq i - 1, s_x = g_x$$

Similarly, let S_{ij} be the subset of S_i in which the ith state variable has value j, or

$$s \in S_{ij} \text{ iff } s \in S_i \text{ and } s_i = j$$

Furthermore, we restrict the set of states of a problem to those that are *solvable* in the sense that:

$$\forall s \in S, \exists \text{ a macro m s.t. } m(s) = g.$$

Definition 2: A *problem instance p* is a pair (P, s_{init}) of a problem **P** and a particular initial state s_{init}.

Definition 3: A *macro* is a finite sequence of operators $(o_1, o_2, \ldots, o_k)$ chosen from **O**, where $k \geq 0$ is the length of the sequence. We write $m(s) = t$ to denote the application of macro **m** to state **s**, where $t = o_k(o_{k-1}(\ldots (o_1(s)) \ldots))$. If k is zero, **m** is the identity macro **I** such that $\forall s \in S, I(s) = s$.

Definition 4: A *macro table* is a set of macros **M**, each denoted by m_{ij} for $1 \leq i \leq n$ and $j \in V$, where m_{ij} is defined as follows:

If $S_{ij} = \emptyset$ then m_{ij} is undefined.

Otherwise, if $S_{ij} \neq \emptyset$, then

$$\forall s \in S_{ij}, m_{ij}(s) \in S_{i+1}$$

Note that if $j = g_i$, then $m_{ij} = I$, the identity macro.

We now address the issue of operator decomposability, starting with a special case called *total decomposability*. The more general case of *serial decomposability* will be covered in the next section.

6.3.2 Total Decomposability

Definition 5: A function **f** is *totally decomposable* iff there exists a corresponding scalar function *f* from *V* to *V* such that

$$\forall\, s \in S,\, \mathbf{f}(s) = \mathbf{f}(s_1, s_2, \ldots, s_n) = (f(s_1), f(s_2), \ldots, f(s_n)).$$

Lemma 6: A macro **m** is totally decomposable if each of the operators in it are totally decomposable.

Proof: In order to prove this result, it suffices to show that the composition of two totally decomposable functions is totally decomposable.

Assume that **g** and **h** are totally decomposable functions and that **f** is the composition of **g** and **h**. Then

$$\mathbf{f}(s) = \mathbf{g}(\mathbf{h}(s)) = \mathbf{g}(\mathbf{h}(s_1, s_2, \ldots, s_n)) = \mathbf{g}(h(s_1), h(s_2), \ldots, h(s_n)) =$$
$$(g\,(h(s_1)), g\,(h(s_2)), \ldots, g\,(h(s_n)))$$

where *g* and *h* are the scalar functions which correspond to **g** and **h**, respectively. Thus, **f** is totally decomposable. □

Definition 7: A problem **P** is totally decomposable if $\forall\, o \in O$, **o** is totally decomposable.

The following theorem is the fundamental result of this section.

Theorem 8: If a problem is totally decomposable, then there exists a macro table for the problem.

Proof: To prove the existence of a macro table **M**, it must be shown that for each *i* and *j*, m_{ij} is either undefined or exists according to definition 4. Hence, $\forall\, ij$ for $1 \leq i \leq n$ and $j \in V$, either:

Case 1: $S_{ij} = \emptyset$ in which case m_{ij} is undefined, or

Case 2: $S_{ij} \neq \emptyset$ in which case $\exists\, s \in S_{ij}$. Since all states are solvable by definition, there exists a macro **m** s.t. **m**(s) = **g**. Recall that

$$\forall\, s \in S_{ij},\, s_y = g_y \text{ for } 0 \leq y \leq i - 1 \text{ and } s_i = j$$

Also, recall that $\mathbf{g} = (g_1, g_2, \ldots, g_n)$. Since $s \in S_{ij}$, **m**(s) = **g**, and **m** is totally decomposable, then

$$m(s_y) = m(g_y) = g_y \text{ for } 0 \leq y \leq i - 1 \text{ and } m(s_i) = m(j) = g_i$$

where *m* is the scalar function corresponding to **m**. This is true independent of the values of s_{i+1} through s_n. Therefore,

$$\forall\, s \in S_{ij},\, m(s_y) = g_y \text{ for } 0 \leq y \leq i$$

Thus, $\quad\quad \forall\, s \in S_{ij},\ m(s) \in S_{i+1}$

Hence, **m** is m_{ij}. $\square$

All of the operators of Rubik's Cube are totally decomposable. As a result, all macros for the cube are totally decomposable as well. This explains why each column of the macro table need only have enough entries for the different possible values of the corresponding state variable, and hence why the total number of macros is small relative to the size of the space.

6.3.3 Serial Decomposability

The small number of macros in the macro table is due to the fact that the effect of the macros is independent of the succeeding variables in the solution order. However, independence of the preceding variables in the solution order is not necessary, since these values are known when the macros are generated. This suggests that a weaker form of operator decomposability would still result in the same number of macros. This is the case with the Eight Puzzle, the Think-a-Dot problem, and the Towers of Hanoi problem.

In the Eight Puzzle, the state variables correspond to the different tiles, including the blank. Each of the four operators (Up, Down, Left, and Right) affect exactly two state variables, the tile they move and the blank. While the *effects* on each of these two tiles are decomposable, the *preconditions* of the operators are not. Note that while there are no preconditions on any operators for Rubik's Cube, i.e. all operators are always applicable, the Eight Puzzle operators must satisfy the precondition that the blank be adjacent to the tile to be moved and in the direction it is to be moved. Thus, whether or not an operator is applicable to a particular tile variable depends on whether the blank variable has the correct value. In order for an operator to be totally decomposable, the decomposition must hold for both the preconditions and the postconditions of the operator.

How do we cope with operators that are not totally decomposable? One possibility is that for those columns of the macro table preceding the one corresponding to the blank tile, we include a separate macro for each possible combination of positions for the tile to be moved and the blank. For those stages following the positioning of the blank, we need only enough macros for the different positions of the tile to be positioned next. The disadvantage of this approach is that the number of macros in the columns that precede the blank in the solution order increases from order n to order n^2, where n is the number of tiles.

The obvious solution to this problem is to pick the blank tile to be first in the solution order. Then, in all succeeding stages the position of the blank will be known and hence the dependence on this variable will not increase the number of macros. The net result of this weaker form of operator decomposability is that it places a constraint on the possible solution orders that will result in a minimum number of macros. The constraint is that the state variables must be ordered such that 1) at each stage of the solution, the preconditions of each operator depend only on the current and preceding state variables in the solution order, and 2) the effect of each operator on each state variable depends only on that variable and preceding state variables in the solution order. If such an ordering exists, we say that the operators exhibit *serial decomposability*. In the case of the Eight Puzzle, the constraint is simply that the blank must occur first in the solution order.

The following section is a formal treatment of serial decomposability. The presentation exactly parallels that of total decomposability.

Definition 9: A *solution order* is a permutation π of the state variables of a state vector. Since we will never refer to more than one solution order at a time, without loss of generality we will continue to refer to a state as a vector of state variables $(s_1, s_2, \ldots, s_n)$ with the assumption that the order of the subscripts corresponds to the order of the state variables in the solution order under consideration.

Definition 10: A function f is *serially decomposable* with respect to a particular solution order π iff there exists a set of vector functions f_i for $1 \leq i \leq n$, where each f_i is a function from V^i to V, and V^i is the set of i-ary vectors with components chosen from V, which satisfy the following condition:

$$\forall s \in S, f(s) = f(s_1, s_2, \ldots, s_n) =$$
$$(f_1(s_1), f_2(s_1, s_2), \ldots, f_n(s_1, s_2, \ldots, s_n))$$

Lemma 11: A macro m is serially decomposable with respect to a solution order π if each of the operators in it are serially decomposable with respect to π.

Proof: In order to prove this result, it suffices to show that the composition of two serially decomposable functions with respect to a solution order π is also serially decomposable with respect to π.

Assume that g and h are serially decomposable functions with respect to a solution order π, and that f is the composition of g and h. Then

$$m(s) = g(h(s)) = g(h(s_1, s_2, \ldots, s_n)) =$$
$$g(h_1(s_1), h_2(s_1, s_2), \ldots, h_n(s_1, s_2, \ldots, s_n)) =$$
$$(g_1(h_1(s_1)), \ldots, g_n(h_1(s_1), \ldots, h_n(s_1, s_2, \ldots, s_n)))$$

where g_i and h_i are the i-ary vector functions which correspond to g and h, respectively. Hence f is serially decomposable with respect to π. $\square$

Definition 12: A problem P is serially decomposable if there exists a solution order π such that $\forall o \in O$, o is serially decomposable with respect to π.

The following theorem subsumes the case of total decomposability and is the main theoretical result of this monograph.

Theorem 13: If a problem is serially decomposable, then there exists a macro table for the problem.

Proof: To prove the existence of a macro table M, it must be shown that for each i and j, m_{ij} is either undefined or exists according to definition 4. Hence, $\forall i, j$ for $1 \leq i \leq n$ and $j \in V$, either:

Case 1: $S_{ij} = \emptyset$ in which case m_{ij} is undefined, or

Case 2: $S_{ij} \neq \emptyset$ in which case $\exists s \in S_{ij}$. Since all states are solvable by definition, there exists a macro m s.t. $m(s) = g$. Recall that

$$\forall s \in S_{ij}, s_y = g_y \text{ for } 0 \leq y \leq i-1, \text{ and } s_i = j$$

Also, recall that $g = (g_1, g_2, \ldots, g_n)$. Since $s \in S_{ij}$, $m(s) = g$, and m is serially decomposable, then

$$m_y(s_1, s_2, \ldots, s_y) = m_y(g_1, g_2, \ldots, g_y) = g_y \text{ for } 0 \leq y \leq i-1 \text{ and}$$
$$m_i(s_1, s_2, \ldots, s_{i-1}, s_i) = m_i(g_1, g_2, \ldots, g_{i-1}, j) = g_i$$

where m_y and m_i are the y-ary and i-ary functions, respectively, corresponding to m. This is true independent of the values of s_{i+1} through s_n. Therefore,

$$\forall s \in S_{ij}, m_y(s_1, s_2, \ldots, s_y) = g_y \text{ for } 0 \leq y \leq i$$

Thus,

$$\forall\, s \in S_{ij},\; m(s) \in S_{i+1}$$

Hence, m is m_{ij}. $\square$

Note that total decomposability is merely a special case of serial decomposability. It is introduced prior to serial decomposability for pedagogical reasons. In the remainder of this monograph, the term serial decomposability will be used in formal contexts to refer to the general case which includes total decomposability. The term operator decomposability will always refer to the general case.

The Think-a-Dot problem exhibits a much richer form of serial decomposability that results in a complex constraint on the solution order. Roughly, the effect of an operator on a particular gate can depend on the values of the gates above it. This suggests that the solution order must include all the gates at one horizontal level before any of the gates at the next lower level. More exactly, the effect of an operator on a particular gate depends only on the values of all of its "ancestors", or those gates from which there exists a directed path to the given gate. Thus, the constraint on the solution order is that the ancestors of any gate must occur prior to that gate in the order. The serial decomposability structure of this problem is directly exhibited by the directed graph structure of the machine. Note that the serial decomposability of this problem is based on the effects of the operators and not on their preconditions, since there are no preconditions on the Think-a-Dot operators.

An extreme case of serial decomposability occurs in the Towers of Hanoi problem. Recall that the variables correspond to the disks and the values correspond to the pegs. There are six operators, one for each possible ordered pair of source peg and destination peg. The applicability of each of the operators to each of the disks depends upon the positions of all the smaller disks. In particular, no smaller disk may be on the source or destination peg of the disk to be moved. This totally constrains the solution order to be from smallest disk to largest disk. We describe this as a boundary case since it exhibits the maximum amount of dependence possible without increasing the number of macros.

Operator decomposability in a problem is not only a function of the problem, but depends on the particular formulation of the problem in terms of state variables as well. For example, under the dual representation of the Eight Puzzle, where state variables correspond to positions and values correspond to tiles, the operators are not decomposable. The reason is that there is no ordering to the positions such the effect of each of the operators on each of the positions can be expressed as a function of only the previous positions in the order.

We conclude this section with the result that a macro table for a problem contains a solution to every problem instance.

Definition 14: Given a macro table **M**, a *macro sequence* m_s is a sequence of macros from the table of the form

$$m_s = (m_{1j_1}, m_{2j_2}, \ldots, m_{nj_n})$$

Theorem 15: Given a problem **P** and a corresponding macro table **M**,

$$\forall\, s \in S,\ \exists\, m_s \text{ in } M \text{ s.t. } m_s(s) = g$$

Proof: By the definition of a macro table,

$$\forall i\ 1 \leq i \leq n,\ \forall\, s \in S_i,\ \exists\, m_{ij} \text{ s.t. } m_{ij}(s) = s_{i+1}$$

Since

$$\forall\, s \in S,\ s \in S_1 \text{ and } S_{n+1} = \{g\},$$

$$\forall\, s \in S,\ \exists\, m_s = (m_{1j_1}, m_{2j_2}, \ldots, m_{nj_n}) \text{ s.t. } m_s(s) = g. \ \square$$

6.4 The General Theory of Macro Problem Solving

In the above discussion we restricted our attention to problems whose states are described as vectors of state variables, and for which the subgoals are to achieve goal values for the individual state variables. We now consider a generalization of the theory which is independent of any particular state description and which encompasses arbitrary subgoals. This generalization is necessary because there exist problems, such as the Fool's Disk, for which good subgoals are known, but the subgoals are more complex than simply achieving values for particular state variables. In fact, the most efficient strategy known for Rubik's Cube is based on such a set of complex subgoals. This general theory is built upon the theory of the General Problem Solver developed by Newell, Shaw, and Simon.

In the classical GPS theory, a problem space consists of a set of states, with no further structure imposed on the state descriptions. In addition, there are a set of differences or subgoals. If we restrict our attention to the case of a single set of goal states, then each difference can be associated with the set of states for which the corresponding subgoal is satisfied. Given an ordering to the subgoal sets, a hierarchical structure of nested sets can be defined where each set is the intersection of all the previous subgoals. The largest set in this structure is the set of initial states and the smallest is the set of goal states. An additional restriction placed on problems to be solved by GPS is that it must be possible to start anywhere in the problem space and proceed toward the goal set by moving into smaller and smaller containing sets without ever having to move into a larger set from a smaller set.

We adopt this structure with one exception: we do not require the current state to always remain in the current subgoal set or proceed into the next set. However, if we only observe the macro problem solving process between macro applications, this restriction is observed. This is a consequence of the fact that our method can be viewed as a generalization of GPS to include macros.

What additional structure do we have to place on this model to allow macro problem solving to be effective? From the initial state we must be able to apply one of a limited number of macros in order to achieve the first subgoal, or to move into the first subgoal set. Hence, the initial set, which is the entire problem space, must be partitionable into a small number of subsets or blocks, such that for any state within a particular block, the single macro corresponding to that block can be applied to that state with the result that the state will be mapped into the next subgoal set. The number of blocks of the partition equals the number of macros in the first column of the macro table. Similarly, the set corresponding to the first subgoal must be partitionable into a small number of blocks so that a single macro will map any member of the same block into the next subgoal set. There must exist such a partition for each subset of the problem space corresponding to a particular subgoal.

Note that the only restriction placed on these partitions is that the number of blocks they partition a set into be small, relative to the size of the set. In particular, there is no requirement that the blocks be of the same size or structure. Furthermore, partitions of different subsets are not constrained to be related in any way, structurally or otherwise.

The restricted form of our theory in terms of vectors of state variables is a special case of this more general formulation. The overall decomposition of the problem space into sets of subgoals is based on the number of state variables whose values are known. The largest set is the entire space. The next subgoal set contains all those states in which the first variable in the solution order is equal to the target value at that stage. The next subset consists of those states for which the first two variables are equal to their respective target values at the next stage, and similarly for the rest. The partition of each subset is based on the different possible values of the next state variable at that stage. For example, at the first stage, the entire space is partitioned into blocks such that for all the states in the same block, the first state variable has the same value. The number of blocks equals the number of possible values of the variable. Similarly, the partition of the next subset is based on the values of the second state variable in the solution order, etc.

The advantage of the general theory over this special case is twofold: First, it is not constrained by any particular structural description of a state in the problem space. Secondly, it allows the macro technique to be used in combination with arbitrarily complex differences, such as those developed by Goldstein's program and related techniques. In general, such differences or subgoals may be expressed in terms of complicated functions of the state components.

6.5 Conclusions

We have presented a theory of the Macro Problem Solver that explains why the technique is effective for the example problems and characterizes the range of problems for which it is useful. A necessary and sufficient condition for the success of the method is that the primitive operators of the problem space be decomposable. If the operators are totally decomposable, then any solution order results in a small number of macros, while serially decomposable operators constrain the solution orders that result in a small number of macros. In addition, an important generalization of the method is based on the two observations that the target values of the state variables need not be their goal values, and that they need not remain constant from one stage to the next. Finally, a general theory of macro problem solving is presented that applies to arbitrary state descriptions and arbitrarily complex subgoals.

7 Performance Analysis

We have seen several example problems for which the Macro Problem Solver is effective, techniques for learning the macros have been presented, and a theory of why the method works has been developed. We now turn our attention to an analysis of the performance of the method. The goal of this exploration is to be able to characterize quantitatively how well macro problem solving works.

7.1 Summary of Methodology and Results

There are three obvious criteria for gauging the performance of this method: the number of macros required to fill the macro table, the amount of time necessary to learn the macros, and the number of primitive moves required to solve an instance of the problem. We will analyze each of these factors in turn.

Since the values of these quantities will depend on the problem, they must be expressed in terms of some problem-dependent parameter. In traditional computational complexity theory, this parameter is often the "size" of the problem, which roughly corresponds to the number of primitive components of the problem. In our case, the number of state variables would correspond to the size of the problem.

Our analysis, however, will not be based on the size of the problem but rather on different measures of the "difficulty" of the problem. For example, the number of primitive moves required for a solution will be expressed as a function of the optimal number of moves. There are two reasons for this approach. One is that the analysis is tractable in this model and produces interesting results. This is due to the fact that the performance of our method is more intimately related to the difficulty of the problem than to the size of the problem. The second reason for adopting this approach is that it allows realistic comparisons with other problem solving strategies for the same class of problems, and with optimal solutions.

Three main results will be presented:

- The number of macros is equal to the *sum* of the number of values for each of the state variables, as compared with the number of states in the space which is the *product* of the number of values for each of the state variables.

- The total learning time is of the same order as the time required to find a single solution using conventional search techniques.

- The length of the solution is no greater than the optimal solution length times the number of state variables. In addition, an average case analysis of solution length is presented that correlates well with experimentally observed values for the 2x2x2 Rubik's Cube. Furthermore, for the Eight Puzzle and the 3x3x3 Rubik's Cube, the solution lengths are approximately equal to or less than those of human strategies.

7.2 Number of Macros

The usefulness of the Macro Problem Solver is based on the fact that an efficient strategy for a very large number of problem instances can be implemented with a very small number of macros. Hence, the actual number of macros required for a given macro table is of obvious interest. This is also a measure of the amount of knowledge required by the strategy, or the amount of space that must be used by the problem solving program.

7.2.1 Number of Macros Related to Size of Space

We begin with some preliminary definitions and lemmas.

Definition 1: An operator o is *applicable* to a state s iff $o(s) \neq s$.

A macro $m = (o_1, o_2, \dots, o_k)$ is *applicable* to a state s iff

$$\forall i \, 1 \leq i \leq k, \, o_i(o_{i-1}(\dots(o_1(s))\dots)) \neq o_{i-1}(\dots(o_1(s))\dots)$$

Definition 2: A function f is *information preserving* iff

$\forall s, t \in S$ s.t. f is applicable to s and t,
$f(s) = f(t)$ implies $s = t$.

Lemma 3: A macro is information preserving if each of the operators in it are information preserving.

Proof: In order to prove this result, it suffices to show that the composition of two information preserving functions is information preserving.

Assume that **g** and **h** are information preserving functions and let **g∘h** be the composition of **g** with **h**. By definition, $\forall$ s,t $\in$ **S** s.t. **g∘h** is applicable to **s** and **t**, **h** is applicable to **s** and **t**, and **g** is applicable to **h(s)** and **h(t)**. Assume that

$$g(h(s)) = g(h(t))$$

Since **g** is information preserving and is applicable to **h(s)** and **h(t)**,

$$h(s) = h(t)$$

Similarly, since **h** is information preserving and is applicable to **s** and **t**,

$$s = t$$

Thus,

$$\forall s,t \in S, \text{ s.t. } g{\circ}h \text{ is applicable to } s \text{ and } t,$$
$$g(h(s)) = g(h(t)) \text{ implies } s = t$$

Therefore, **g∘h** is information preserving. □

Definition 4: A problem **P** is information preserving iff $\forall$ **o** $\in$ **O**, **o** is information preserving.

Lemma 5: If **f** is a total information preserving function from a domain **D** to a range **R**, and **D**∩**R** = ∅, then |**R**| ≥ |**D**|, where |**R**| is the cardinality of the set **R**.

Proof: Assume |**R**| < |**D**|. Since every element of **D** must be mapped to some element of **R**, then by the pigeon-hole principle,

$$\exists x,y \in D, x \neq y \text{ s.t. } f(x) = f(y)$$

Furthermore, since **D**∩**R** = ∅,

$$\exists x,y \in D \text{ s.t. } f(x) \neq x \wedge f(y) \neq y \wedge f(x) = f(y) \wedge x \neq y$$

But this contradicts the assumption that **f** is information preserving. Hence, |**R**| ≥ |**D**|. □

Definition 6: A problem **P** is *connected* iff

$$\forall s,t \in S, \exists \text{ a macro } m \text{ s.t. } m(s) = t$$

Note that connectedness is a stronger property than solvability since it requires a path between every pair of states as opposed to just a path from every state to the

73

goal. The reader can easily verify that all of our example problems are information preserving and connected. The following theorem is the main result of this section.

Theorem 7: Given a problem **P** that is connected, serially decomposable, and information preserving, then for all macro tables for **P**,

$$|S| = \prod_{i=1}^{n} |M_i| \text{ where } M_i = \{m_{ij} \mid S_{ij} \neq \emptyset\}$$

Proof: The proof is by induction on n, the number of state variables in the problem.

Basis Step: Assume $n = 1$. Then $|S|$ is the number of different possible values for the single state variable. For each of these values, there exists a unique macro to map it to the goal value, including the identity macro, and there are no other macros in the macro table. Hence,

$$|S| = |M_1| = \prod_{i=1}^{n} |M_i| \text{ for } n = 1$$

Induction Step: Assume that the theorem is true for all problems with up to n state variables and consider problems with $n + 1$ state variables. Since the S_{1j} sets are mutually exclusive and collectively exhaustive,

$$|S| = \sum_{j \in V} |S_{1j}| = \sum_{S_{1j} \neq \emptyset} |S_{1j}|$$

Since **P** is connected,

$$\forall j, k \in V \text{ s.t. } S_{1j} \neq \emptyset \wedge S_{1k} \neq \emptyset,$$
$$\exists s \in S_{1j}, t \in S_{1k}, \text{ and } m \in O^\times \text{ s.t. } m(s) = t$$

where $O^\times$ is the set of all finite sequences of operators from **O**. Since **P** is serially decomposable,

$$\forall s \in S_{1j}, \ m(s) \in S_{1k}$$

If $j = k$, then

$$|S_{1k}| = |S_{1j}|$$

Otherwise, if $j \neq k$, then

$$S_{1k} \cap S_{1j} = \emptyset$$

and since **m** is information preserving,

$$|S_{1k}| \geq |S_{1j}|$$

Since j and k are completely symmetric in the above argument, we can interchange them to yield

$$|\mathbf{S}_{1j}| \geq |\mathbf{S}_{1k}| \text{ and hence } |\mathbf{S}_{1j}| = |\mathbf{S}_{1k}|$$

Therefore,

$$\forall j,k \text{ s.t. } \mathbf{S}_{1j} \neq \emptyset \wedge \mathbf{S}_{1k} \neq \emptyset, \; |\mathbf{S}_{1j}| = |\mathbf{S}_{1k}| = |\mathbf{S}_{1g_1}|$$

Since all of the $\mathbf{S}_{1j}$ sets are the same size,

$$\sum_{\mathbf{S}_{1j} \neq \emptyset} |\mathbf{S}_{1j}| = x \cdot |\mathbf{S}_{1g_1}|$$

where x is the number of values of j for which $\mathbf{S}_{1j} \neq \emptyset$. But that is just $|\mathbf{M}_1|$. Therefore,

$$|\mathbf{S}| = \sum_{\mathbf{S}_{1j} \neq \emptyset} |\mathbf{S}_{1j}| = |\mathbf{M}_1| \cdot |\mathbf{S}_{1g_1}|$$

However, $\mathbf{S}_{1g_1}$ is the set of states for which the first state variable equals its goal value. After mapping the first state variable to its goal value, the problem that remains is isomorphic to a problem with one less state variable. Hence, by the inductive assumption,

$$|\mathbf{S}_{1g_1}| = \prod_{i=2}^{n} |\mathbf{M}_i|$$

Thus,

$$|\mathbf{S}| = |\mathbf{M}_1| \prod_{i=2}^{n} |\mathbf{M}_i| = \prod_{i=1}^{n} |\mathbf{M}_i| \quad \square$$

In other words, the total number of states in the problem space is equal to the *product* of the number of macros in each column. This includes the identity macro in each column in the row corresponding to the goal value of that variable. By comparison, the total number of macros is only the *sum* of the number of macros in each column of the macro table. Thus, in general, the number of macros will equal only a small fraction of the total number of states.

7.2.2 Minimizing the Number of Macros

What is the theoretical minimum number of macros required to solve a problem? Note that each decomposition of the state into a set of state variables corresponds to a factoring of the total number of states into factors which are the numbers of possible values for each variable, given that the values of the previous variables in the solution order have been determined. The number of macros is the sum of these factors. Hence we can restate the problem of finding the minimum number of macros as the following problem: given a fixed value, how can it be factored so that the sum of the factors is a minimum?

Definition 8: A *factorization* F of an integer $n \geq 2$ is a sequence of integers

$$(f_1, f_2, \ldots, f_k) \text{ s.t. } \forall i \ 1 \leq i \leq k, \ f_i \geq 2 \text{ and } \prod_{i=1}^{k} f_i = n.$$

Definition 9: Given an integer $n \geq 2$, a *minimal sum factorization* $H = (h_1, h_2, \ldots, h_j)$ is a factorization of n such that for all factorizations $F = (f_1, f_2, \ldots, f_k)$ of n,

$$\sum_{i=1}^{j} h_i \leq \sum_{i=1}^{k} f_i$$

Lemma 10:

$$\forall x \geq 2, y \geq 2, \quad xy \geq x + y$$

Proof: Since $x \geq 2$ and $y \geq 2$,

$$\exists a \geq 0 \text{ s.t. } x = 2 + a \text{ and } \exists b \geq 0 \text{ s.t. } y = 2 + b$$

$$xy = (2 + a)(2 + b) = 4 + 2a + 2b + ab$$

$$x + y = (2 + a) + (2 + b) = 4 + a + b$$

$$xy - (x + y) = a + b + ab$$

Since $a \geq 0$ and $b \geq 0$,

$$a + b + ab \geq 0$$

$$xy - (x + y) \geq 0$$

$$xy \geq x + y \quad \square$$

Theorem 11: The prime factorization of a number is a minimal sum factorization.

Proof: All factorizations of a number can be generated by multiplying pairs of numbers starting from the prime factorization. However, by the above lemma, no such multiplication can decrease the total sum. Hence, the prime factorization must be a minimal sum factorization.

Unfortunately, while this achieves the theoretical minimum, there is no guarantee that a problem can be decomposed to this extent while still preserving operator decomposability. The above result does imply, however, that whenever a state variable can be divided into two or more variables without violating operator decomposability, the result will be a reduction in the total number of macros (except for a variable with four values, which results in an equal number of macros). For example, consider the 2x2x2 Rubik's Cube macro table in Appendix A2. Each state variable encodes both the position and orientation of a particular cubie. However, the position and orientation information for each cubie could be represented by two separate variables, provided that the position variable precedes the orientation variable in the solution order for each cubie. This is because the effect of a macro on the orientation of a cubie depends on the position of that cubie. In other words, while the original formulation of the problem is totally decomposable, separating position and orientation into two separate variables makes the problem only serially decomposable.

The resulting macro table is shown in Appendix A5. In this strategy, the position and orientation of each cubie are satisfied in two separate stages. Note that while the original macro table contains 75 non-identity macros, by separating position and orientation into distinct variables, the number of non-identity macros is reduced to 33.

7.3 Learning Time

In addition to the number of macros required to fill the macro table, the amount of time required to learn the macros is an important performance parameter of the macro problem solving technique.

To address this issue, we assume that we have the computational resources to search to a sufficient depth to find all the macros and hence the macro composition technique is not required. We also will assume that each primitive operator has a primitive inverse. Recall that all the macros are acquired during a single search of the problem space starting at the goal node. Thus, the learning time depends primarily on the branching factor of the space and the depth to which the search must go. The execution of the learning program is interleaved with that of the problem solver so that the learning program only runs when a new macro is required. This ensures that the learning program will only search to a depth necessary to find all macros.

We begin with a set of definitions aimed at capturing the depth of search required to find all macros.

Definition 12: The *distance* between two states is the shortest length macro that maps one state to another, or

$$\forall\, s,t \in S \text{ s.t. } \exists\, m \in O^{\times} \text{ s.t. } m(s) = t, \; d(s,t) = \operatorname*{MIN}_{m(s)=t} L(m)$$

where $n(m)$ is the length of macro m, or the number of primitive operators in **m**.

Definition 13: The *diameter* of a problem P is the maximum distance between any pair of connected states, or

$$\operatorname*{MAX}_{s,t \in S} d(s,t)$$

Definition 14: The *radius* of a problem P with respect to the goal state g is the maximum distance to the goal state or

$$D_P = \operatorname*{MAX}_{s \in S} d(s,g)$$

For most problems, including all of our examples, the radius of the problem for all goal states will equal the diameter. However, the radius for some goal states could be less than the problem diameter for some problems.

Definition 15: A *subgoal* is a set of states. A given state is said to satisfy a subgoal iff it is an element of the set. The particular subgoals we are concerned with here are the sets

$$S_i \text{ for } 1 \le i \le n + 1$$

Recall that

$$S_1 = S \text{ and } S_{n+1} = \{g\}$$

Definition 16: Given two subgoals S_1 and S_2, the *subgoal distance* is the maximum distance from any state in S_1 to the closest state in S_2, or

$$D(S_1, S_2) = \operatorname*{MAX}_{s \in S_1} \operatorname*{MIN}_{t \in S_2} d(s,t)$$

Definition 17: Given a sequence of subgoals $(S_1, S_2, \ldots, S_n, S_{n+1})$, the *maximum subgoal distance* D_s is

$$D_s = \operatorname*{MAX}_{1 \le i \le n} D(S_i, S_{i+1})$$

Given a set of subgoals, the maximum subgoal distance is a better measure of the "difficulty" of a problem than the problem radius. In general, D_s will be less than D_P. A useful analogy here is that of crossing a stream on stepping stones. The difficulty of the problem is related to the maximum distance between stepping stones and not the width of the river.

We now formally define the inverse of an operator and the inverse of a macro.

Definition 18: The *inverse* of a function f is a function f^{-1} s.t.

$$\forall s \in S \text{ s.t. } f \text{ is applicable to } s, \ o^{-1}(o(s)) = s$$

Lemma 19: For any macro $m = (o_1, o_2, \ldots, o_k)$, the macro

$$m^{-1} = (o_k^{-1}, o_{k-1}^{-1}, \ldots, o_1^{-1})$$

is the inverse of **m**.

Proof: Instead of providing the details of a formal inductive proof, we will simply show that $g^{-1} \circ f^{-1}$ is the inverse of $f \circ g$. By the definition of f^{-1},

$$\forall s \in S \text{ s.t. } f \text{ is applicable to } s, \ f^{-1}(f(s)) = s$$

substituting g(s) for s,

$$\forall s \in S \text{ s.t. } f \text{ is applicable to } g(s), \ f^{-1}(f(g(s))) = g(s)$$

applying g^{-1} to both sides,

$$\forall s \in S \text{ s.t. } f \text{ is applicable to } g(s),$$
$$g^{-1}(f^{-1}(f(g(s)))) = g^{-1}(g(s))$$

By the definition of g^{-1},

$$\forall s \in S \text{ s.t. } f \text{ is applicable to } g(s) \text{ and } g \text{ is applicable to } s,$$

$$g^{-1}(f^{-1}(f(g(s)))) = s$$

Since the applicability of g to s and f to g(s) implies that $f \circ g$ is applicable to s, $g^{-1} \circ f^{-1}$ is the inverse of $f \circ g$. $\square$

We now turn our attention to the branching factor of a problem space.

Definition 20: Given a state $s \in S$, we define the *branching factor b (s)* as

$$\forall s \in S, b(s) = |\{t \text{ s.t. } t \in S \wedge t \neq s \wedge \exists o \in O \text{ s.t. } o(s) = t\}|$$

Definition 21: Given a problem in which each operator has an inverse, the *maximum branching factor* for a problem P is defined as

$$B_m = \underset{s \in S}{\text{MAX}} \ b(s) - 1$$

The one is subtracted to exclude the immediate ancestor of a given state in the branching factor.

Definition 22: Given a problem in which each operator has an inverse, we define the *average branching factor* as

$$B_a = \sum_{s \in S} (b(s) - 1) / |S|$$

In other words, the average branching factor of a search space is the average number of states that can be reached by the application of a primitive operator from any given state in the space, excluding the given state and its immediate ancestor. The branching factor of a space can usually be determined by examining the set of operators. For example, if there are no preconditions on the operators, as in Rubik's Cube, then the branching factor is approximately the number of primitive operators.

If there are preconditions, then we compute a weighted average of the number of operators applicable for each set of preconditions, weighted by the probability of that set of conditions occurring. For example, consider the Eight Puzzle. If the blank is in the center position, there are four applicable operators, one of which must be the inverse of the last operator applied. If the blank is in a corner, there are two operators with one being the inverse of the last operator. Finally, if the blank is in the middle of a side, three operators are applicable, one of which is the inverse of the last operator. Ignoring the inverse of the last operator, and assuming that every position of the blank is equally likely, the average branching factor of the space after the first move is $1/9 \cdot 3 + 4/9 \cdot 1 + 4/9 \cdot 2 = 15/9$ or 1.67.

We continue our analysis with the definition of an optimal macro table.

Definition 23: An *optimal macro table* for a problem P is a complete macro table M in which each macro is the shortest possible macro that could occupy that slot in the table. Formally,

$$\forall m_{ij} \in M, m \in O^{\times}, \text{ if } \forall s \in S_{ij}, m(s) \in S_{i+1}, \text{ then}$$
$$L(m) \geq L(m_{ij})$$

In order to simplify the complexity analysis of the learning task, we will analyze the tree-search bi-directional search instead of the hashing scheme. While it is easier to analyze and its complexity is of the same order as the hashing algorithm, the constant factors of this algorithm are larger and hence it is less efficient. We repeat the statement of the algorithm below.

A breadth-first search of the problem space is performed starting from the goal state. As each state is generated, it is stored in a search tree where each level of the tree corresponds to a different state variable and different nodes at the same level correspond to different possible values for that state variable. The ordering of levels of the tree from top to bottom corresponds to the solution order of the state variables from first to last. Thus, each node of the tree corresponds to an assignment of values to an initial subsequence of state variables in the solution order.

A state is inserted in the tree by filtering it down from the root node to the last existing node which corresponds to a previously generated state. A new node is created at the next level of the tree and the macro which generated the new state is stored at the new node. Since the states are generated breadth-first, this ensures that with each existing node is stored a shortest macro which maps the goal state to the initial subsequence of values corresponding to the node.

When a new state reaches the last previously existing node while being inserted in the tree, a composite macro is created as follows. If i is the level in the tree, $\mathbf{a}$ is the existing macro, and $\mathbf{b}$ is the new macro, then the macros $\mathbf{a} \circ \mathbf{b}^{-1}$ and $\mathbf{b} \circ \mathbf{a}^{-1}$ are created. Since the states that result from applying $\mathbf{a}$ and $\mathbf{b}$ to the goal state match in the first $i-1$ state variables, both these composite macros are guaranteed to leave the first $i-1$ variables of the goal state invariant. To determine what value of the ith state variable would be mapped to the goal value, we apply the inverse of each of the these macros, which is the other member of the pair, to the goal state and note the resulting value of the ith state variable. If the corresponding entry of the macro table is empty, it is filled with the new macro. Otherwise, the new macro is discarded.

The following theorem is the main result of this section.

Theorem 24: Given a serially decomposable problem $\mathbf{P}$ for which each primitive operator has an inverse primitive operator, an optimal macro table $\mathbf{M}$ for $\mathbf{P}$ can be generated in time $O(nD_sB_m{}^{D_s/2})$, where n is the number of state variables, B_m is the maximum branching factor of the space, and D_s is the maximum subgoal distance for the solution order embodied in the macro table **M**.

Proof: For $1 \le i \le n$, the optimal macro for m_{ig_i} is the identity macro. Optimal macros which are only one move long can also be treated as special cases since there are at most B_m of them. For all other optimal macros m_{ij} where $j \ne g_i$, we can divide the sequence of operators into two parts and label them **a** and **b**. Since $\mathbf{a} \circ \mathbf{b} = m_{ij}$,

$$\forall x \ 1 \le x \le i-1, \ \mathbf{a}_x \circ \mathbf{b}_x \, (g_1, g_2, \ldots, g_x) = g_x \text{ and}$$
$$\mathbf{a}_i \circ \mathbf{b}_i \, (g_1, g_2, \ldots, g_{i-1}, j) = g_i$$

Thus,

$$\exists \mathbf{v} \in V^i, \ \mathbf{v} = (v_1, v_2, \ldots, v_i) \text{ s.t. } \forall x \ 1 \le x \le i-1,$$

$$\mathbf{b}_x \, (g_1, g_2, \ldots, g_x) = v_x \text{ and } \mathbf{a}_x \, (v_1, v_2, \ldots, v_x) = g_x \text{ and}$$

$$\mathbf{b}_i \, (g_1, g_2, \ldots, g_{i-1}, j) = v_1 \text{ and } \mathbf{a}_i \, (v_1, v_2, \ldots, v_i) = g_i$$

Since m_{ij} is an optimal macro, each operator must change each state it is applied to, or else that operator could be removed from the macro to create a shorter macro with the same effect. This together with the fact that each operator has an inverse implies that each subsequence of m_{ij} has an inverse. In particular,

$$\exists \mathbf{a}^{-1} \in O^\times \text{ s.t. } \forall x \ 1 \le x \le i, \ \mathbf{a}_x^{-1} \, (g_1, g_2, \ldots, g_x) = v_x$$

Thus,

$$\forall x \ 1 \le x \le i-1, \ \mathbf{b}_x(g_1, g_2, \ldots, g_x) = v_x = \mathbf{a}_x^{-1} \, (g_1, g_2, \ldots, g_x)$$

Therefore, each optimal macro m_{ij} can be decomposed into two parts which, when applied to the goal state, generate states which match in their first $i-1$ components.

Following the above argument in reverse order shows that the converse is also true: Given two macros **b** and $\mathbf{a}^{-1}$ which when applied to the goal state generate states which match in the first $i-1$ components, then $\mathbf{a} \circ \mathbf{b}$ leaves the first $i-1$ components of the goal state invariant. If the resulting value of the ith state variable is j when the macro is applied to the goal state, then the inverse macro will map j to g_i. Since our problem is serially decomposable,

$$\forall \mathbf{m} \in O^\times, \text{ if } \exists s \in S_{ij} \text{ s.t. } m(s) \in S_{i+1}, \text{ then } \forall s \in S_{ij},$$
$$m(s) \in S_{i+1}$$

Hence, $\mathbf{m} = m_{ij}$.

Dividing a macro as close to in half as possible minimizes the length of the longest part. Thus, a search to depth $\lceil D/2 \rceil$ suffices to find all macros up to length D. Since the subgoal distance $D(S_1, S_2)$ is the maximum length macro required to map *any* element of S_1 to *some* element of S_2, and the maximum subgoal distance, D_s, is the maximum of these values for the sequence of subgoals in the solution order, D_s is equal to the longest macro in an optimal macro table. Thus, the search must proceed to depth $\lceil D_s/2 \rceil$. Since B_m is the maximum branching factor for any node except the root node, the total number of nodes generated in the breadth-first search is $O(B_m{}^{D_s/2})$, since the branching factor of the root node and the extra .5 generated by the ceiling function can both be absorbed in the constant coefficient.

Generating each state requires an operator to be applied which we assume requires $O(n)$ operations. Inserting a state into the search tree also requires $O(n)$ operations since there are n levels to the tree. Creating the composite macros requires $O(nD_s)$ operations since $D_s/2$ operators must be applied to compute the effect of the inverse of the macros on the goal state to determine the correct row for the macros.

Thus, the total amount of time to generate an optimal macro table is

$$O(nD_sB_m{}^{D_s/2}) \quad \square$$

Note that in practice, the maximum branching factor B_m can usually be replaced by the average branching factor B_a. The necessary condition is that after a short initial search, the expected branching factor of a state be equal to the average branching factor.

How does this compare with the the running time of a standard problem solving program trying to solve a particular instance of the problem? We assume the problem solver uses the same set of subgoals with the same ordering and can perform bi-directional search as well, but has no additional knowledge about the problem. In other words, the problem solving program is given the same information about the problem as the learning program. Using an ordinary search with subgoals, the problem solver performs a bi-directional search between the initial state and the first subgoal, then performs another bi-directional search between the first subgoal and the second subgoal, and continues similarly until the final goal is reached. The running time of this algorithm is dominated by the depth of the longest search, which is D_s. Hence, the total running time is $O(nD_sB_m{}^{D_s}/2)$. The learning program requires only a single search to depth D_s. Thus, the runtime of the learning program which learns an efficient strategy for solving all instances of the problem is of the same order as that of a standard problem solving program, using the same knowledge, that solves just one problem instance!

7.4 Solution Length

So far, we have considered the amount of knowledge required to solve our example problems and the amount of time necessary to acquire that knowledge. We now turn our attention to the quality of the resulting solutions. In particular, we will analyze the lengths of the solutions generated by the macro problem solver in terms of the number of primitive moves. We will first consider the worst-case solution length, then the average case based on a given macro table, and finally the expected solution length independent of any particular macro table. In addition, typical solution lengths generated by human problem solvers will be considered.

For problems such as Rubik's Cube and the Eight Puzzle, the problem radius, D_P, is only known for versions of the problem small enough to allow exhaustive search of the entire state space. Thus, optimal solution lengths have been determined experimentally for the 2x2x2 Rubik's Cube (11 moves) and the Eight Puzzle (30 moves [Schofield 67]) but are not known for the 3x3x3 cube or the Fifteen Puzzle. It follows that all known algorithms for these problems, other than exhaustive search, may yield suboptimal solution paths. A lower bound on the problem radius is the depth in the search tree, starting from the goal node and using the average branching factor, at which the number of nodes first exceeds the number of states in the problem space.

We define solution length as follows.

> **Definition 25:** Given a macro sequence m_s, we define the solution length as the total number of primitive operators, or
> $$\forall\, m_s \text{ in } M,\ L(m_s) = \sum_{i=1}^{n} L(m_{ij_i})$$
> where $L(m)$ is the length of macro m.

7.4.1 Worst Case Results

The goal of worst-case analysis is to determine the maximum solution length that could be generated to solve some problem instance.

Theorem 26: The worst-case solution length is equal to the sum of the subgoal distances for the given solution order, or

$$\underset{s \in S}{MAX}\, L(m_s) = \sum_{i=1}^{n} D(S_i, S_{i+1})$$

Proof:

$$\underset{s \in S}{MAX}\, L(m_s) = \sum_{i=1}^{n} \underset{m_{ij}}{MAX}\, L(m_{ij})$$

However, by the definition of subgoal distance,

$$\forall i\ 1 \le i \le n,\ \underset{m_{ij}}{MAX}\, L(m_{ij}) = D(S_i, S_{i+1})$$

Therefore,

$$\underset{s \in S}{MAX}\, L(m_s) = \sum_{i=1}^{n} D(S_i, S_{i+1}) \quad \square$$

Two weaker corollaries follow immediately from this result.

Corollary 27:

$$\forall s \in S,\ L(m_s) \le n \cdot D_s$$

where D_s is the maximum subgoal distance for the solution order.

Proof: From the above theorem, we know that

$$\forall s \in S,\ L(m_s) \le \sum_{i=1}^{n} D(S_i, S_{i+1})$$

By the definition of D_s,

$$\forall i\ 1 \le i \le n,\ D(S_i, S_{i+1}) \le D_s$$

Thus,

$$\sum_{i=1}^{n} D(S_i, S_{i+1}) \le \sum_{i=1}^{n} D_s = n \cdot D_s$$

Therefore,

$$\forall s \in S,\ L(m_s) \le n \cdot D_s \quad \square$$

Corollary 28:

$$\forall s \in S,\ L(m_s) \le n \cdot D_P$$

where D_P is the radius of the problem **P** with respect to the goal state **g**.

Proof: From the above corollary, we know that

$$\forall\, s \in S, \ L(m_s) \leq n \cdot D_s$$

By the definition of D_P, $D_s \leq D_P$. Thus,

$$\forall\, s \in S, \ L(m_s) \leq n \cdot D_P \quad \square$$

Note that given an optimal macro table, the Macro Problem Solver solutions are the optimal solutions that pass through the given set of subgoals. This is due to the fact that each of the individual macros are optimal. The reason that these solutions are not optimal in the global sense is that the global optimal solution need not pass through the given subgoals.

For the 2x2x2 Rubik's Cube, $D_S = D_P = 11$ moves. Since there are 6 non-empty columns of the macro table, this produces a worst case bound of 66 moves. Summing the lengths of the longest macros in each column for the macro table in Appendix A2 reveals an actual worst case solution length of 38 moves. This is due to the fact that the maximum length macro in each column except the last is less than 11 moves long.

7.4.2 Experimental Average-Case Results

While the goal of worst-case analyses is to bound the longest possible solution length, average case analysis is concerned with the actual solution length for a particular problem, averaged over all problem instances. In order to do an average case analysis, some assumption must be made about the distribution of problem instances. We assume that all possible problem instances are equally likely.

> **Definition 29:** Since we assume that all possible initial states are equally likely, we define the *average-case solution length* L_A to be the solution length for each particular initial state averaged over all possible initial states, or
>
> $$L_A = \sum_{s \in S} L(m_s) / |S|$$

> **Lemma 30:** Given a macro table for a problem **P** which is connected and information preserving, there exists a bijection from **S** to **M**, where **M** is the set of macro sequences from the macro table for **P**.
>
> **Proof:** By theorem 7, we know that

$$|S| = \prod_{i=1}^{n} |M_i|$$

Since

$$|M| = \prod_{i=1}^{n} |M_i|, \text{ then } |S| = |M|$$

By theorem 15 in chapter 6, there exists a total mapping from **S** to **M**. Since **P** is information preserving and all the macros are applicable to their respective states,

$$\forall \, s, t \in S, \ m_s(s) = m_s(t) \text{ implies } s = t$$

Hence, the mapping is one-to-one. Therefore, the mapping is a bijection. □

Theorem 31: Given a problem that is connected and information preserving, the average case solution length is equal to the sum of the average macro length in each column of the macro table, or

$$L_A = \sum_{i=1}^{n} \sum_{j \in V} L(m_{ij})/|M_i|$$

Proof: By definition,

$$L_A = \sum_{s \in S} L(m_s)/|S|$$

Since there is a bijection from **S** to **M**,

$$\sum_{s \in S} L(m_s)/|S| = \sum_{m_s \in M} L(m_s)/|S|$$

If we let x_{ij} be the number of times that m_{ij} appears in an element of **M**, then

$$\sum_{m_s \in M} L(m_s)/|S| = \sum_{i=1}^{n} \sum_{j \in V} x_{ij} \cdot L(m_{ij})/|S|$$

Since **M** is the set of all possible macro sequences,

$$\forall \, ij \ x_{ij} = \prod_{k \neq i} |M_k| = \prod_{k=1}^{n} |M_k|/|M_i| = |S|/|M_i|$$

Therefore,

$$L_A = \sum_{i=1}^{n} \sum_{j \in V} (|S|/|M_i|) \times (L(m_{ij})/|S|) =$$

$$\sum_{i=1}^{n} \sum_{j \in V} L(m_{ij})/|M_i| \quad \square$$

For the 2x2x2 Rubik's Cube macro table in Appendix A2, the average solution length is 27 moves. This is significantly less than the 38 move worst-case solution length from the same table.

Note that this result depends on the particular solution order chosen for the macro table, as does the worst-case result. In order to factor out this variable, average case solution lengths were computed for 25 randomly generated solution orders for the 2x2x2 Rubik's Cube. These solution lengths were then averaged and the result was 28.39 moves with a maximum variation from the smallest to the largest of 9.8 percent.

7.4.3 Analytical Average-Case Results

Under certain assumptions, we can also predict analytically what the average case solution length will be, independent of any particular solution order. The basic idea is that since the first subgoal only constrains the value of the first state variable, there will be many states in the space that satisfy the first subgoal and hence we would expect to have to examine only a small number of states before finding one. Similarly, since the second subgoal constrains the first two state variables, we would expect to look at a few more states in order to find one satisfying this subgoal, and similarly for the third subgoal, etc.

To make this idea precise, note that given the number of different values for the first state variable, we can compute the probability that any given state will satisfy the first subgoal. This gives us the expected number of states that would have to be examined before finding such a state. Then, given the number of new states that are generated at each depth in the search, we can compute the expected depth of search required to find a state satisfying the subgoal. The same computation is then repeated for the first two state variables, the first three, etc.

This analysis is based on the assumption that the states are randomly distributed throughout the problem space, without any particular bias. For example, we assume that two states that match in all but one state variable are no closer together in the space than any two random states. The data reported in Table 2-3 suggest that this assumption is fairly accurate in the case of the 2x2x2 Rubik's Cube.

We quantify this analysis in the definitions and theorem below.

   Definition 32: The *average subgoal distance* $D_A(S_i, S_{i+1})$ is the average over all states in S_i of the distance to the closest state in S_{i+1}, or

$$D_A(S_i, S_{i+1}) = \sum_{s \in S_i} \underset{t \in S_{i+1}}{\text{MIN}} \; d(s,t)/|S_i|$$

Definition 33: A sequence of subgoals $(S_1, S_2, \ldots, S_{n+1})$ is *uncorrelated* if

$$\forall i \; 1 \leq i \leq n, \; D_A(S_i, S_{i+1}) = D_A(S, S_{i+1})$$

or in other words, the states in successive subgoals are no closer together on the average than any arbitrary states in the problem space.

Definition 34: The *expected solution length* for a problem **P** is

$$\sum_{k=0}^{D_P} k \cdot P(k)$$

where k is a solution length, D_P is the radius of the problem, and $P(k)$ is the probability that given an arbitrary problem instance, the macro sequence which solves it is of length k.

Theorem 35: Given a problem **P** and a macro table based on an uncorrelated sequence of subgoals, the expected solution length is

$$\sum_{i=2}^{n+1} \sum_{d=0}^{D_P} d \cdot ((1 - P_i)^{L_d} - (1 - P_i)^{N_d + L_d})$$

where P_i is the probability that a given state is an element of S_i, N_d is the average number of states that first occur at a distance d from any given state, and L_d is the average number of states that occur at a distance less than d from any given state.

Proof: First, note that

$$\forall i \; 1 \leq i \leq n+1, \; P_i = |S_i|/|S|$$

Let $P_{id}(S_{i-1})$ be the probability that given a state in S_{i-1}, the closest state in S_i is at distance d. Since we assume that successive subgoals in the solution order are uncorrelated,

$$\forall i \; 1 \leq i \leq n+1, \; P_{id}(S_{i-1}) = P_{id}(S) = P_{id}$$

The probability of finding a state in S_i at a distance d or less is one minus the probability of not finding it, or

$$\sum_{k=1}^{d} P_{ik} = 1 - (1 - P_i)^{N_d + L_d}$$

Similarly, the probability of finding a state in S_i at a distance less than d is

$$\sum_{k=1}^{d-1} P_{ik} = 1 - (1 - P_i)^{L_d}$$

Therefore, the probability of first finding a state in S_i at distance exactly d

89

is the probability of finding it at a distance d or less minus the probability of finding it a distance less than d, or

$$\sum_{k=1}^{d} P_{ik} - \sum_{k=1}^{d-1} P_{ik} = P_{id} = (1 - P_i)^{L_d} - (1 - P_i)^{N_d + L_d}$$

The expected length of the $i - 1^{st}$ macro in a macro sequence is the expected distance to first reach a state in S_i from a state in S_{i-1}, or

$$\sum_{d=0}^{D_P} d \cdot P_{id}$$

Therefore, the expected solution length is

$$\sum_{i=2}^{n+1} \sum_{d=0}^{D_P} d \cdot P_{id} = \sum_{i=2}^{n+1} \sum_{d=0}^{D_P} d \cdot ((1 - P_i)^{L_d} - (1 - P_i)^{N_d + L_d}) \quad \square$$

The result of this computation for the 2x2x2 Rubik's Cube is an expected solution length of 28.73 moves, independent of any particular macro table or solution order. This is within 1.2 percent of the experimental average solution length of 28.39 moves, computed by averaging the average solution lengths for 25 different macro tables.

7.4.4 Comparison with Human Strategies

This section compares the average solution lengths generated by the Macro Problem Solver with solution lengths produced by human strategies for the Eight Puzzle and the 3x3x3 Rubik's Cube. For the Eight Puzzle, Ericsson [Ericsson 76] found that the average solution length generated by ten human subjects on eight different problem instances was 38 moves. This is within 5% of the 39.78 move average case solution length computed from the macro table in Table 4-1. An informal survey of ten people who could solve Rubik's Cube resulted in an average solution length of 125 primitive moves, where a 180 degree twist is counted as a single primitive move. This is significantly longer than the 86.38 move average case solution length based on the macro table of Appendix A3. Thus, we find that for these problems, solutions generated by the Macro Problem Solver are close to or superior to those of humans in terms of number of primitive moves.

7.5 Conclusions

We have analyzed the performance of the macro problem solver along three different dimensions: the number of macros, the learning time, and the length of solution. In each case, we compared the performance measure to some measure of the "difficulty" of the problem, including number of states in the space, time to search for a single solution, and optimum solution length, respectively. We found that:

- Whereas the number of states is the product of the number of values for each state variable, the number of macros is the sum of these same quantities.

- The learning time is of the same order as the time required to search for a single solution using standard techniques.

- The solution lengths are less than or equal to the optimal solution length times the number of state variables. In addition, we were able to predict analytically average case solution lengths independent of solution order, and achieved very good agreement with experimentally determined values in the case of the 2x2x2 Rubik's Cube. Furthermore, for the Eight Puzzle and the 3x3x3 Rubik's Cube, we found that the average solution length is, respectively, very close to and less than the solution lengths generated by human problem solvers.

Numerical values of these measures for the example problems are summarized in Table 7-1.

Table 7-1: Experimental performance measures for example problems

PROBLEM	$Dist_p$	$Dist_s$	Len_a	Len_w	macros	learn
Eight Puzzle	30	14	39.78	64	35	*
Fifteen Puzzle	>65	24	139.40	214	119	:10
2x2x2 Rubik's Cube	11	11	27.00	38	75	:18
3x3x3 Rubik's Cube	>18	12	86.38	134	238	14:28
Tower of Hanoi (3 disks)	7	3	7.33	11	6	*
Think-a-Dot	9	4	7.50	15	7	*

LEGEND

$Dist_p$ problem radius or maximum distance to goal state
$Dist_s$ maximum distance between successive subgoals
Len_a average case solution length for Macro Problem Solver
Len_w worst case solution length for Macro Problem Solver
macros   number of non-identity macros in macro table
learn   the amount of time in seconds to learn macros
       using bi-directional search
* less than one second

8 Reflections and Further Work

This chapter presents some reflections on this work, and suggests some directions for further research along these lines. Further work includes reducing solution lengths and learning time by selection of solution orders and target values, and combining macro problem solving with other problem solving methods such as operator subgoaling, macro generalization, and problem decomposition. A measure of problem difficulty is proposed, based on the branching factor of the problem space and the length of the largest gap between two successive subgoals. In addition, macro-operators are viewed as a general representation for knowledge, taking examples from theorem proving, computer programming, and road navigation. Finally, the use of macros for representing knowledge in arbitrary problem spaces is considered, along with the notion of learning by searching for macro-operators.

8.1 Reducing Solution Length and Learning Time

Two important parameters to the macro learning program are the solution order, or the sequence in which the state variables are mapped to their target values, and the actual set of target values themselves. For some problems, the choice of solution order and/or target values can have a large impact on the efficiency of the resulting solution and learning time.

8.1.1 Solution Order Selection

As demonstrated in chapter 6, in order to generate a macro table with a minimum number of macros, the solution order is constrained by the serial decomposability of the operators. More precisely, the solution order must be such that the applicability and the effect of any operator on any given state variable depends only on that state variable and previous ones in the solution order. For some problems, such as the Towers of Hanoi, this condition totally constrains the solution order and no further selection is possible. However, for other problems, such as Rubik's Cube, operator decomposability places no constraints on the solution order and hence it must be selected by other means. For problems such as the Eight Puzzle and Think-a-Dot, the solution order must be selected within the constraints imposed by operator decomposability.

For the 2x2x2 Rubik's Cube, 25 different solution orders were randomly generated and the average case solution length was computed for each of the resulting macro tables. The variation among these solution lengths was less than ten percent, implying that for this problem the choice of solution order has very little effect on the efficiency of the resulting solution. However, for problems such as the Eight Puzzle this is not the case. A macro table was generated for the Eight Puzzle based on the solution order [0 2 6 4 8 1 5 3 7], which was deliberately chosen to result in an inefficient solution strategy. The average number of primitive moves required to solve an instance of the problem using this macro table is 58.06 as compared with the 39.78 moves required using the macro table in Table 4-1.

For most problems, the solution order will affect the efficiency of the resulting solutions; the 2x2x2 Rubik's Cube is an anomaly in this respect. Unfortunately, one cannot predict a priori what solution order will result in the most efficient solution strategy. Rather, heuristics must be used to select a solution order which will result in a reasonably efficient strategy. Such a heuristic was used to determine the solution order for the 3x3x3 Rubik's Cube.

The heuristic is to select a solution order such that at any point in the order, if we assume that the previous problem components are fixed and not allowed to change, the mobility of the remaining problem components is maximized. The heuristic is applied as follows. First, the binary matrix shown in Table 8-1, using the Eight Puzzle as an example, is constructed. The rows correspond to the positions of the tiles and the columns correspond to the primitive operators, represented by the pair of positions they affect, ignoring the direction of the move. The matrix contains a one in every element where the operator associated with the column affects the position associated with the row.

94

Table 8-1: Operator-position incidence matrix for Eight Puzzle

OPERATORS

		1-2	1-8	2-3	2-B	3-4	4-B	4-5	5-6	6-B	6-7	7-8	8-B
	B	0	0	0	1	0	1	0	0	1	0	0	1
	1	1	1	0	0	0	0	0	0	0	0	0	0
P	2	1	0	1	1	0	0	0	0	0	0	0	0
O S	3	0	0	1	0	1	0	0	0	0	0	0	0
I T	4	0	0	0	0	1	1	1	0	0	0	0	0
I O	5	0	0	0	0	0	0	1	1	0	0	0	0
N S	6	0	0	0	0	0	0	0	1	1	1	0	0
	7	0	0	0	0	0	0	0	0	0	1	1	0
	8	1	0	0	0	0	1	0	0	0	0	0	1

Given this matrix, a solution order is generated by first selecting a position that is affected by a minimum number of operators, in this case a corner position, and the tile which occupies that position in the goal state becomes the first variable in the solution order. Next, all the columns (operators) which affect that position are deleted from the matrix and again a position affected by the minimum number of remaining operators is selected. Ties are resolved by selecting positions adjacent to those already selected, and ties still remaining are resolved arbitrarily. This process is continued until the entire solution order is determined. In the case of the Eight Puzzle, one solution order generated by this algorithm, depending on how the arbitrary choices are resolved, is [B 1 2 3 4 5 6 7 8].

Note that this is not the only possible technique for generating solution orders. Another idea[1] is to determine the solution order dynamically during the macro learning phase, based on the state variables that are left invariant by the shortest macros. Further research is needed to evaluate these and other methods with

---

[1] suggested by Bruce Lucas

respect to the efficiency of the solution strategies they generate and the efficiency of learning the macros.

8.1.2 Target Value Selection

In addition to solution order, another parameter of the Macro Problem Solver that can effect solution efficiency and learning time is the target values to which the state variables are mapped in the intermediate states of the solution. As shown in chapter 6, these target values need not be the goal values until the final macro is applied.

In fact, these extra degrees of freedom in the macro table allow us to construct slightly more efficient strategies for some problems than those generated by using goal values as targets for the intermediate states. Table 8-2 shows another macro table for the Eight Puzzle. This macro table is based on intermediate target values (shown in table 8-3) that are different from the goal values at some points. For example, after the 1 tile has been placed in the upper left hand corner, if the 2 tile is placed in its goal position next to it, in general it will have to be moved in order to get the 3 tile to its position. A better strategy is to place the 2 tile in the 3 position, then the 3 tile can be placed below it, and both tiles can be "rotated" into their goal positions. The same strategy is followed in the case of the 4 and 5 tiles. Another technique is to leave the blank in the 4 position after the 2 and 3 tiles are correctly placed, instead of returning it to the center. Similarly the blank is left in the 6 position after the 4 and 5 tiles are placed. Both these techniques are incorporated into the macro table in Table 8-2, with a consequent slight decrease in the average number of moves required for solution, from 39.78 to 39.14.

The reason the difference is so small is that whenever any target value changes from one subgoal to the next, the chance of not having to apply any macro at that stage is lost, and hence the average solution length tends to increase. However, the point of this example is to demonstrate that goal target values do not necessarily result in the most efficient solutions.

Another example is provided by the Towers of Hanoi problem. In Chapter 4 we found that using goal values for the target values resulted in an inefficient solution

96

Table 8-2: More efficient macro table for Eight Puzzle

POSITIONS	TILES 0	1	2	3	4	5	6
0					RULDR		D
1	UL						
2	U	RDLU	LDRU	DRUULLDRRDLLU			
3	UR	DLURRDLU					
4	R	LDRURDLU	DLUR	DLU		LDRRUULDRDLLUUR	
5	DR	ULDRURDLDRUL	LURDDLUR	LURDDLU	R		
6	D	URDLDRUL	ULDRDLUR	ULDRDLU	URD	LUR	
7	DL	RULDDRUL	URDLULDRDLUR	URDLULDRDLU	URRDLLURD	URDLLUR	RDL
8	L	DRUL	RDLULDRRUL	RULLDRDLU	RRULDLURD	RULDLUR	DRULD

The average case solution length is 39.14 moves.

Table 8-3: Target values for Eight Puzzle macro table

SOLUTION STAGE	TILES 0	1	2	3	4	5	6	7	8
0	0								
1	0	1							
2	0	1	3						
3	4	1	2	3					
4	0	1	2	3	5				
5	6	1	2	3	4	5			
6	0	1	2	3	4	5	6		

strategy for this problem. The macro table for the 3-disk problem in Table 4-3 requires 11 moves to solve the problem from the standard initial state in which all disks are stacked on one peg, while the optimal strategy only requires 7 moves. In fact, 11 moves is the worst case solution length for the macro table and 7.3 moves is the average case, while 7 moves is the worst case solution length for the optimal strategy.

By changing the target values, we can generate a macro table that produces the optimal solution for any given initial state. For example, the macro table in Table 8-4 is based on the same goal state (all disks on peg C), and the target peg for the smallest disk in the first column is peg C, but the target peg for the two smallest disks in the second column is peg B. This macro table produces the optimal solution for the initial state where all disks are on peg A, but its average case and worst case solution lengths are identical to those of the macro table in Table 4-3.

Table 8-4: Macro table for three disk Towers of Hanoi problem

		DISKS		
		1	2	3
P E G S	A	AC	AB CB	AC BA BC AC
	B	BC	CB	BC BA CA BC AB AC BC
	C		CA CB AB	BA BC AC

Can we build a macro table for the Towers of Hanoi problem that produces the optimal solution for all initial states? The answer is no, not with a small number of macros. The reason is that the optimal target peg for a given disk depends on the positions of all the larger disks. For example, in order to move the largest disk from its source peg to its destination peg, the second largest disk should be targeted for the "other" peg, that which is neither the source nor the destination peg of the largest disk. Similarly, the optimal target for the next smallest disk depends on the source and destination of the next larger disk, which depends on the next larger disk, etc. The problem is that the positions of the larger disks are not known when the macros are generated because the solution order constrains us to position the disks in order of increasing size.

In general, the selection of target values and their effect on overall solution efficiency is an area that requires further study.

8.1.3 Simultaneous Subgoal Satisfaction

One final technique for improving the efficiency of solutions generated by the Macro Problem Solver is simultaneous subgoal satisfaction. In the examples so far, we have tried to decompose a problem into as many subgoals as possible in order to minimize the number of macros and the depth of search required to learn them. However, by solving two or more state variables simultaneously, the number of moves required to solve them both will in general be less than the sum of the moves necessary to solve each one individually. The penalty is that the number of macros required increases sharply since the number of macros needed to solve two state variables simultaneously is the product of the number needed to solve them individually. The limiting case of this technique is solving all the state variables at once, in which case the number of macros equals the number of states in the space and the solution lengths are globally optimal.

8.2 Combining Macro Problem Solving with Other Methods

So far, the Macro Problem Solver has been presented in isolation as a complete problem solving method. However, in reality this method is simply another addition to a collection of existing tools for general problem solving. It is natural to ask how well this new technique can be integrated or combined with the existing stock of ideas to solve problems that no single method could solve alone. In fact, the Macro Problem Solver can easily be integrated with other problem solving techniques such as operator subgoaling, macro generalization, and problem decomposition.

8.2.1 Operator Subgoaling

The basic idea of operator subgoaling is that at a given state of a problem, if an operator which is effective for achieving the next intermediate state in the problem is not applicable, then a subgoal is set up to satisfy the preconditions of the operator. A classic example of operator subgoaling occurs in the Towers of Hanoi problem. If an intermediate goal is to move the largest disk from its current peg to its goal peg but there are smaller disks on top of it, then it cannot be moved. The solution is to set up a subgoal of clearing the top of the largest disk so that it can be moved.

Banerji [Banerji 83] generalizes the notion of operator subgoaling to include subgoals which make an existing operator *effective* for solving a subgoal rather than simply *applicable*. For example, in Rubik's Cube, all operators are always applicable so there is no need for subgoals to establish the preconditions of an operator. However, in general an operator will only be effective in solving a subgoal under certain conditions. This gives rise to subgoals of establishing these *effectiveness conditions*.

Operator subgoaling can also be used with the Macro Problem Solver. As described so far, the method requires a complete macro table such that at each point in the solution process, there exists a separate macro which will map the next state variable to its target value from each possible value it may have. However, a complete macro table is unnecessary.

Assume that the macro table is incomplete and hence there is an empty slot in the table which corresponds to a legal value for that state variable at that stage of the solution. Thus, when we get to that stage of the solution, if the corresponding state variable has the value corresponding to the empty slot, we set up the subgoal of mapping the state variable to one of the values for which we have a macro which will map it to its target value. This subgoal would be achieved by applying one of the other macros in the same column of the table. The result is that the total number of macros that must be stored is reduced at the expense of a longer overall solution length, since two or more macro applications may be required to map a single state variable to its target value.

This is equivalent to the macro composition technique except that it is applied at problem solving time instead of learning time. Human cube solvers, and particularly novices, make extensive use of this technique since it drastically reduces the number of macros they must learn and remember.

8.2.2 Macro Generalization

As described so far, a macro is a fixed sequence of explicitly named primitive operators which can only fill a unique location in the macro table. However, another technique for reducing the number of distinct macros that must be stored in the table is to generalize macros so that the same generalized macro can be used in more than one slot in the macro table. This technique was used extensively in the work on MACROPS for the STRIPS system [Fikes 72].

One way of generalizing a macro is to take advantage of symmetries of the problem. For example, in Rubik's Cube, the macro (U2 R2 U2 R2 U2 R2) is very similar to the macro (F2 D2 F2 D2 F2 D2), and in fact to 22 other macros which consist of three repetitions of a 180 degree twist of one side followed by a 180 degree twist of an adjacent side. This entire class of macros could be represented by the *parameterized macro* $M(x,y) = (x2\ y2\ x2\ y2\ x2\ y2)$, where x and y are constrained to be adjacent faces. Similarly, in macros for the Think-a-Dot and Towers of Hanoi problems, the actual names of input channels and pegs, respectively, could be replaced with variables under appropriate conditions.

Another way of generalizing macros is suggested by the Eight and Fifteen Puzzles. If we relax the assumption that the position of the blank tile must be fixed between macro applications, then the same sequence of Left, Right, Up, and Down moves could be applied starting from different positions of the blank, and hence with different effects.

In fact, the extent to which Eight and Fifteen Puzzle macros can be generalized is suggested by the fact that an expert strategy for these problems can be built from only two macros: one that moves a single tile in any direction by repeatedly maneuvering the blank back in "front" of the tile, and another macro that completes a row by rotating the last two tiles into position. However, a general description of either of these macros would be relatively complex. For example, the macro for moving a single tile must be able to use any side of the tile to move the blank back in front due to the constraints of the boundaries and not moving previously positioned tiles. Similarly, the row completion macro must work for both horizontal and vertical rows.

8.2.3 Problem Decomposition

This work began with the observation that some problems could not be solved by satisfying a sequence of subgoals one at a time without ever violating a previously satisfied subgoal. However, there may be a *set* of subgoals such that once every subgoal in the set is satisfied, the rest of the problem can be solved without violating any subgoal in the set. For example, in the Eight Puzzle, once the top row is correctly positioned, then the remainder of the the problem can always be solved without ever disturbing this completed row. Such a problem is called *block decomposable*.

This idea is known as problem decomposition and is at the heart of the General Problem Solver. The value of this technique is that once a set of subgoals is satisfied, all operators that violate any of these subgoals are deleted from the set of primitive operators, and hence the branching factor for the remainder of the search is reduced. The disadvantage is that the resulting solution may be less efficient than a solution generated without protecting subgoals.

The way to combine this powerful problem decomposition method with the Macro Problem Solver is first to divide the solution order into as many intervals as can be solved sequentially as sets of state variables without violating previously solved sets. Then the macro learning program is used to generate a macro table for each of these subsequences individually, but using only those primitive operators that do not affect any of the previously solved subsequences. In other words, the problem is first decomposed as far as possible into sets of subgoals that are serializable, and then the Macro Problem Solver is used to solve each set of subgoals independently. For example, a complete decomposition of the Eight Puzzle could separate the tiles into the sets {1}, {2,3}, {4,5}, and {6,7,8}. Similarly, a complete decomposition for the Think-a-Dot problem could separate the gates into the sets {1}, {2,4,6}, and {3,5,7,8} [Banerji 80].

The fact that the combination of these two methods is significantly more powerful than either is alone is demonstrated by the full 3x3x3 Rubik's Cube. Recall from Chapter 5 that the bi-directional search for cube macros left seven empty slots in the macro table when memory was exhausted. These slots were filled by the macro composition technique, with the penalty that the resulting macros were not the shortest macros for the job. However, by first solving a 2x2x2 subcube on the corner of the full cube, the remainder of the cube can always be solved without ever disturbing the 2x2x2 subcube, even within a macro. In other words, the remainder of the cube can always be solved by twisting only the remaining three faces.

The resulting macro table is shown in Appendix A6. The four movable cubies of the 2x2x2 subcube are solved using twists of all six faces while the remaining sixteen cubies are solved by twisting only the three faces which do not affect the 2x2x2 subcube. Note that some of the macros are fifteen moves long. This extra depth of search is made possible by the reduced branching factor which results from removing the primitive operators that twist three of the faces. The average solution length for this macro table is 100 primitive moves which is slightly more than the 89 moves for the macro table without the decomposition.

It is surprising to most human solvers that the full Rubik's Cube can be decomposed in this way. This suggests that discovering such a decomposition for a problem, if one exists at all, is a non-trivial task in general. The heuristic that was used to suggest this decomposition was the same as that used for generating solution orders, namely pick a set of state variables such that the freedom of the remaining state variables is maximized. Clearly, finding such problem decompositions is an area which requires further research.

8.3 A Measure of Problem Difficulty

It is natural to ask what features of a problem ultimately limit the performance of the macro learning program, even when combined with a good decomposition of the problem into sets of independent subgoals. Recall that both the time and space complexity of the macro learning program are dominated by the exponential term $B^{D_s/2}$ where B is the average branching factor of the problem space and D_s is the longest macro necessary to get between two successive intermediate states. If we assume that the problem solver has this set of subgoals available and no additional knowledge about the problem, then this quantity also appears to be a good intuitive measure of problem difficulty as experienced by other problem solving programs and human problem solvers. While further work would be required to support or refute this claim, we advance it here as a plausible conjecture.

In evaluating this proposal, it is worthwhile to examine several competing measures. One relates the difficulty of a problem to the size of the problem space. However, problem size is not a good intuitive measure of problem difficulty because there exist problems in large spaces for which there are short solutions which are easy to find. For example, if we take the physical disks and pegs of the Towers of Hanoi problem but remove the restrictions of moving one disk at a time and never placing a larger disk on top of a smaller one, then we are left with an easy problem with a solution length of at most two moves, one for moving the disks from each of the non-goal pegs. However, the problem space is even larger than that of the standard Towers of Hanoi problem since the disks on a peg are not constrained to be in order according to size.

This suggests that a better measure of problem difficulty is the optimal solution length in terms of number of primitive moves. The trouble with this hypothesis is that there exist problems for which the solution path is long but which require few if any choices along the way. For example, there are several puzzles, such as the Chinese Rings problem, for which the problem graph is a single large cycle with a branching factor of one after the first move. Such problems are not difficult to solve if the bookkeeping is done carefully, even though they may be time consuming. As another example, most "drudgery" jobs such as adding up long columns of numbers have this property.

Perhaps an analogy mentioned previously is useful here. Consider the problem of crossing a stream on stepping stones. The size of the stream, its length times its width, is analogous to the size of the problem space, and the width of the stream corresponds to the length of the minimum solution path. The stepping stones are analogous to intermediate states or subgoals. Clearly the length of the stream is irrelevant to the difficulty of crossing it. Similarly, the width of the stream is not that important if there are sufficient stepping stones. The critical factor which determines the difficulty of crossing the stream is the spacing between the stepping stones, and in particular the maximum distance between an adjacent pair of stones on the easiest path.

As another analogy, one is reminded of the two watchmakers, Hora and Tempus, in Simon's *Sciences of the Artificial* [Simon 69]. Both make watches from 1000

104

different pieces which fall apart when the watchmaker must answer the phone. However, Hora's watches are constructed from ten stable assemblies, each of which is composed of ten stable subassemblies of ten pieces each, while Tempus' watches have no stable assemblies or subassemblies. As a result, Hora can complete many more watches than Tempus in spite of the same number of interruptions. The analogy is between the number of pieces that must be assembled to make up a stable subassembly and the number of moves that must be made to get from one subgoal to the next.

The value of subgoals for problem solving depends on the maximum distance between successive subgoals being less than the total solution length. In other words D_s must be less than D_P. This is true regardless of whether the subgoals are serializable or not. The reason for protecting satisfied subgoals when possible is based on two factors: one is that it makes it much more likely that the distance between subgoals will be less than the total solution length, and second, it reduces the branching factor for the remainder of the search. Both of these factors improve the efficiency of problem solving and learning.

Our experiments have shown that for some problems, such as the 3x3x3 Rubik's Cube, even without the benefit of independent subgoals which can be solved sequentially, the maximum distance between successive subgoals (12 moves) is still significantly less than the optimal solution length (greater than 17 moves). This implies that by solving these subgoals, progress toward the solution is being made, even though the subgoals do not remain solved. In other words, while the subgoals are not independent, the degree of dependence among them is limited.

Related evidence can be found in the work of Goldberg [Goldberg 79] on NP-complete problems. Goldberg showed that the average-case performance of a relatively simple algorithm for boolean satisfiability is of order N^2. The fact that this problem is NP-complete in the worst case is related to the fact that there are no known subproblems, such as satisfying assignments to subsets of the variables, that are guaranteed to represent progress toward a total solution. However, Goldberg's result suggests that by carefully making partial variable assignments, with a capability for backtracking on failure, these intermediate states do in fact represent progress toward the goal on the average.

In summary, two ideas have been presented in this section. One is that for a given decomposition of a problem into subgoals, the branching factor of the space, raised to half the power of the maximum distance between successive subgoals, is an appropriate measure of problem difficulty. The second is that even when such a set of subgoals is not serializable, they often represent progress toward the main goal, to the degree that the maximum distance between two successive subgoals (D_S) is less than the total solution length (D_P).

8.4 Macros as a Representation for Knowledge

It is almost a cliche of artificial intelligence that expert problem solving performance in a domain comes only as a result of a great deal of knowledge about the domain [Newell 82]. Clearly, the Macro Problem Solver exhibits expert behavior in the domain of the example problems. Where then is the knowledge? The knowledge is contained in the macro-operators which make up the macro table.

If macro-operators are an effective representation of knowledge in these domains, can knowledge in other domains be represented as macros as well? In this section we will explore the use of macro-operators as a representation for knowledge in several other domains. First, we will examine in detail the domains of road navigation and Euclidean problem spaces in general. Next, we will consider the use of macros to represent knowledge about arbitrary problem spaces. Finally, we will briefly touch on the domains of theorem proving and computer programming. For purposes of this discussion, we will depart from the restricted case of macros as used by the Macro Problem Solver, and refer to macros as more general operator sequences.

8.4.1 Road Navigation

The problem of road navigation is how to get from one point on a network of streets to another. This problem has been studied by Kuipers [Kuipers 78, Kuipers 77] and by Elliot and Lesk [Elliot 82]. The states of the space are intersections between streets and the operators are the streets themselves, which take a traveller from one intersection to another. But what do we define as the primitive operators? We adopt the principle that a primitive operator is one that maps one legal state into another without passing through intermediate states from which other operators could be applied. Thus, in the case of road navigation, a primitive operator is a move between two adjacent intersections. For example, a section of street one block long serves as a primitive operator as does a section of interstate highway between two successive interchanges. Note that this definition results in a very large number of primitive operators, of the same order as the number of states. However, for an arbitrary road network, there is no more economical description than simply to list all the intersections and the connections between them.

Two different types of macros are used in road navigation. One is the routes that individuals remember for frequently made trips, such as between home and work. The second is named roads, which are macros used by an entire population of people to navigate in an area.

8.4.1.1 Individual Macros

An immediate observation about human problem solving in this space is that most of it is not problem solving at all but simply recall of stored solutions. For example, to get from home to work and back, most people do not plan a new route each day but rather follow a path that has been learned and remembered. Similarly, most short trips in the vicinity of a person's home or work are accomplished by recall of stored routes. In fact, it is probably the case that for most people, most of their road navigation is accomplished by remembering learned paths.

These paths are clearly macro-operators, since they are sequences of primitive operators, often quite long, which are learned and stored. They are a very effective representation for knowledge about how to get from one place to another in an area a person is familiar with.

The value of storing these macros comes from the fact that for any given individual, all possible trips in an area are not equally likely. Rather, certain trips, such as between home and work, occur very frequently. Hence, it is computationally economical to store the macros for these trips since the cost of learning and remembering them can be amortized over a large number of uses.

However, what if we expand our perspective beyond a single traveller to include an entire population? When considering the set of trips made by the entire population of an area, we would expect the frequency distribution of all possible trips by a large population to more closely approximate a uniform distribution than that for an individual. Note that even for a population the distribution will not be uniform. For example, trips to and from places with high concentrations of people, such as large office buildings or even cities, will be more frequent. However, it is a good approximation when compared with the set of trips made by an individual. Are macros still useful in this situation?

8.4.1.2 Named Roads as Macro-Operators

When we look at a road network, what we find in addition to intersections and streets connecting them is that certain sets of contiguous streets between intersections, usually straight but not always, are given the same names. In fact, almost all street sections are a part of some uniformly named road. Furthermore, most motorists tend to follow these roads in the sense that at any given intersection, most automobiles leave the intersection on the road with the same name as that on which they entered the intersection.

Given our definition of a primitive operator as a section of street between two adjacent intersections, then these commonly named roads are macro-operators since they are sequences of primitive operators. They are "stored" both on road maps and in the actual environment in the form of street signs.

While most roads are straight sections of streets, the view of a named road as a macro-operator becomes clearer when one considers certain types of non-standard roads. For example, when a state or federal highway passes through a town, it often follows a tortuous path with many turns while maintaining its name. Furthermore, in such a situation, the same section of road will often carry the names of several different highways plus a local name as well. As another example, when construction closes a section of a road, a detour that joins the two severed ends of the road and carries the same name is usually "constructed" by simply posting signs. In fact, roads are often "built" by just posting signs. A prime example of this are the beltways that surround Pittsburgh (e.g. the Blue Belt). These roads were created by linking together existing sections of major secondary roads with

108

road signs to mark each of the many turns. Roads such as U.S. Route 1, which goes from the eastern border of Maine to Key West and includes the main street of almost every city and town in between, were also built by connecting together existing sections of highway.

An alternative to this model of a named road as a macro-operator views a road as the result of a sequence of streets projected at a higher level of abstraction and ignoring the low level detail of each intersection. However, when one examines a road map drawn at a high level of abstraction, such as a map showing just the U.S. Interstate Highway System, one still finds named roads that pass through more than one intersection. Thus, if the primitive operators are still sections of road between intersections, then named highways are still sequences of primitive operators or macros. The only effect of abstracting to a higher level space is that some macros in the lower level space become primitive operators in the higher level space, and as a result, macros in the higher level space are composed of fewer primitives than they were in the lower level space.

Note that the usefulness of a road is enhanced by the fact that it can be used for a large number of different trips. To be precise, a two-way road can be used to get from any intersection on the road to any other, and a one-way road can be used to go from any intersection to any other in the correct direction. Hence, a road can be viewed as a collection of macros all sharing the same sequence of primitive operators but differing in beginning and end points.

Clearly, one of the reasons that motorists follow named roads is for efficiency or speed of travel. Most roads are straight and a vehicle can go straight through an intersection faster than it can make a turn. However, an equally important reason for the existence of named roads is as a navigational aid. If one knows or is told that a certain road will take them to a certain destination, then at each intersection along that road, and there may be many, the person knows which of several paths to take out of the intersection.

Can we characterize more generally why macros are useful for the problem of street navigation? In other words, what exactly is the value of a given macro-operator in such a space? In order to answer this question, we will generalize the problem space to a continuous Euclidean plane.

109

8.4.2 Macros in Euclidean Problem Spaces

Consider an area with a very dense road network, so dense that we can approximate it by a continuous plane where every point is a state and there exists a primitive operator to go a short distance, relative to the size of the plane, in any direction from any point. A quantity of search in this space is measured by the amount of two-dimensional area covered. The problem is to find a path between two arbitrary points on this plane. We assume that we do not know the relative direction of either point from the other.

The most efficient strategy is to search outward in concentric circles from both endpoints simultaneously, until the circles intersect (see Figure 8-1). If the distance between the two points is D, the circles will meet after expanding to a radius of $D/2$ each, assuming they expand at the same rate, and the total area covered will be $2\pi(D/2)^2$ or $\pi D^2/2$.

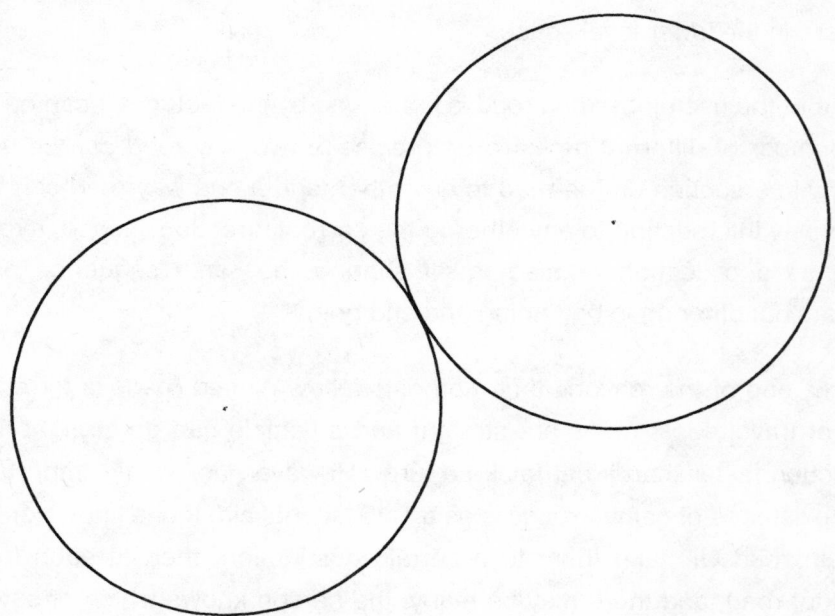

Figure 8-1: Search with no macros

Now assume there is a marked path through the space running east-west, in other words a macro-operator (see figure 8-2). In this case, the searches proceed as before but if one of the searches intersects the path before reaching the other, then it follows the path in both directions until it meets the other search. In that case the total amount of search is $\pi R_1^2 + \pi R_2^2$ where R_1 and R_2 are the perpendicular distances of each endpoint from the path. The path will be useful whenever $R_1^2 + R_2^2$ is less than $D^2/2$.

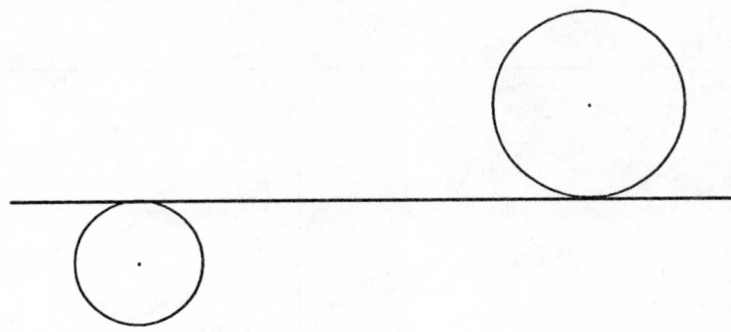

Figure 8-2: Search with one macro

Note that the introduction of a single macro reduces the amount of search for a large number of problem instances, roughly for those pairs of initial and goal states that lie closer to the macro than to each other. However, there is a penalty for this search reduction and that is that the resulting paths are not of optimal length. Any path using this macro will be longer than the optimal path unless both endpoints lie on the path and the path is straight.

An east-west road is of no use for finding a path between two points that are directly north-south of each other. However, if we add a north-south path, and connect it to the east-west path, we reduce the search required for even more problem instances (see Figure 8-3). In general, as we increase the number of connected macros to cover more of the space, the amount of search to solve an arbitrary problem instance becomes $2\pi R^2$, where R is the average distance from a state to the closest macro. This assumes that no search is required within the macro network.

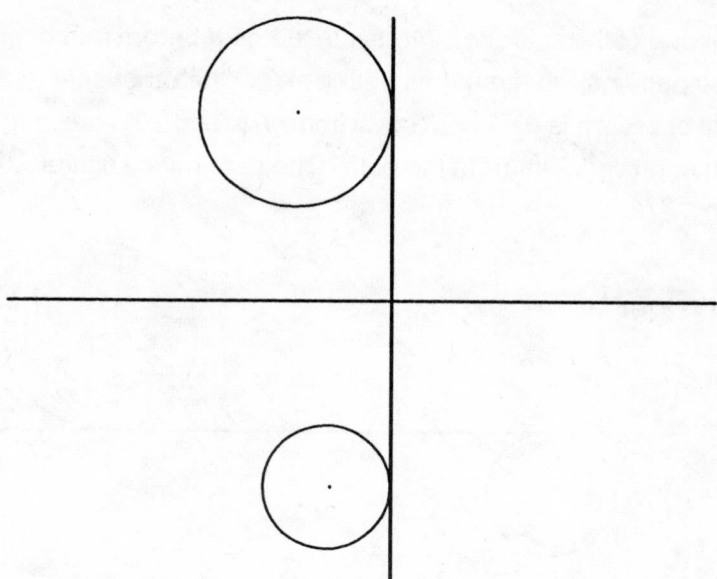

Figure 8-3: Search with two macros

8.4.3 Macros in Arbitrary Problem Spaces

Can we quantify the tradeoff between the size of a macro network and the amount of search required to solve an arbitrary problem instance? Furthermore, can we automatically learn a useful macro network for an arbitrary problem space? In order to answer these questions realistically, we consider an arbitrary discrete problem space.

8.4.3.1 Macro/Search Tradeoff

In order to quantify the macro/search tradeoff, we return to the single-goal model in which every problem instance has a different initial state but the same goal state. We assume that the macro network is connected, that it contains the single goal state, and that it uniformly covers the problem space in the sense that the average distance from a state to the closest macro is roughly constant over the entire space. We further assume that finding a path to the goal from any point on the macro network requires no search. One way of accomplishing this is to mark every macro with the direction to the goal.

112

Let S be the number of states in the space and let M be the size of the macro network expressed as the number of states that are located on a macro. Since we assume that the macros uniformly cover the space, we expect one out of every S/M states in any part of the space to lie on a macro. Thus, if we start from any arbitrary initial state, we would expect to have to search about S/M states before finding a state on the macro network. Hence, the total amount of search is S/M. Note that the product of the number of states in the macro network, M, and the amount of search required to find a path from any arbitrary state to the goal, S/M, equals the number of states in the space, S, independent of the size of the macro network. In other words, there is a multiplicative tradeoff between the size of the macro network and the amount of search required to solve problem instances in the space.

8.4.3.2 Learning Macros in Arbitrary Problem Spaces

Given an arbitrary problem space, how can we learn a macro network which will achieve the above tradeoff? One possibility is to take a random walk starting from the goal state, and store the path as a macro. However, random walks tend to wander around their origins, and hence such a macro is not likely to reach states that are far from the goal. If we bias the random walk by excluding all states that were previously visited, the distance from the origin will gradually increase, but very slowly. Hence, another technique is required.

Note that the most useful macros in a Euclidean problem space are straight line segments. A straight line has the property that the shortest path between any two points on the line is along the line. The analog of a straight line in an arbitrary discrete problem space is a macro with the property that the shortest path between any two states on the macro is along the macro. All the macros considered so far in this work, with the exception of the seven generated for the 3x3x3 Rubik's Cube using macro composition, have this optimality property.

This suggests that a useful macro network for an arbitrary problem graph could be learned by conducting a breadth-first search from the goal state, and storing several macros which have the property that each successive state on each macro is one move further from the goal via the shortest path than the preceding state. Once the depth limit of the search is reached by exhausting the available memory, then similar searches could be sprouted from the ends of each of the macros, and this process could be repeated. A technique such as this may prove to be a useful general learning paradigm.

8.4.4 Macros in Theorem Proving and Computer Programming

We now turn our attention to two real-world problem solving domains, theorem proving and computer programming, and find that much of the knowledge in these domains can be captured in the form of macro-operators.

8.4.4.1 Theorem Proving

Consider the problem of proving theorems in some axiomatized domain such as propositional logic. A state in the problem space is the set of formulas that are known to be true at any given point. The initial state is composed of the axioms of the system plus the antecedent of the theorem to be proved. The goal state is one in which the consequent of the theorem is asserted. The task is to find a sequence of states from the antecedent to the consequent of the theorem. The primitive operators of the space are the rules of inference of the system.

A difficult theorem to prove usually involves a long sequence of applications of axioms and rules of inference. One way in which a theorem prover improves its performance is by learning and remembering theorems which can be used as lemmas to prove other theorems. When a theorem is used as a lemma in a proof, it is simply a shorthand notation for the sequence of individual steps that went into proving the theorem initially. Thus a theorem behaves as a macro-operator when used in a proof.

Knowledge about a domain generally advances by the accumulation of more and more theorems that are proven. These theorems have two purposes. One is that they represent knowledge about the domain for its own sake. The other, and perhaps more important purpose, is that these theorems can be used as lemmas to prove other theorems. These other theorems to be proved may be beyond the capability of the theorem prover without the addition of these lemmas as single deductions. Thus, we find that much of the knowledge in a theorem proving domain can be viewed as macro-operators.

8.4.4.2 Computer Programming

A similar situation exists in the domain of computer programming. The problem of computer programming is to generate a sequence of machine instructions which when run on a computer will implement a particular algorithm. The primitive operators of the space are these machine instructions. In general, a complex program may involve sequences which are thousands of machine instructions long.

One of the early techniques discovered for dealing with this complexity was higher level languages and compilers. A higher level language is a set of programming constructs with the property that in general each construct expands into several lower level machine instructions. (If the correspondence is one-to-one, the language is called an assembly language.) A compiler is provided to perform this translation automatically. Thus, the constructs of a higher level language can be viewed as macro-operators in the space of machine instructions.

The value of these higher level constructs is that they improve the efficiency of the programming process, although in general at a slight cost in efficiency of the resulting programs. The reason for the improvement is that it has been shown empirically that the productivity of a programmer in terms of statements per day is relatively independent of the language. Thus, a programmer coding in a higher level language effectively produces more machine language instructions per day than a programmer in an assembly language. The constructs of a higher level language represent knowledge about programming because they select out those particular sequences of machine instructions, out of all possible sequences, which are likely to be most useful to a programmer.

Note that this process of constructing higher level macro-operators out of sequences of lower level instructions is repeated at many different levels of the programming process. For example, the beginning student of a higher level language learns and stores program schemas which are common patterns of usage of language statements. Similarly, the expert programmer usually writes a set of procedures or subroutines which are appropriate to his application and then writes the rest of the program in terms of these routines. Both these schemas and subroutines are macros constructed from the higher level language, and represent knowledge about a class of programming problems or an application domain.

115

Hence, we find that in computer programming, as in theorem proving, knowledge is often encoded as macro-operators. In fact, the term macro itself is borrowed from a sequence of instructions used in computer programming.

8.5 Conclusions

There are several research directions for extending the work presented in this monograph. One is the automatic seletion of solution orders and target values for the Macro Problem Solver. Another is enhancing the power of the method by combining it with other problem solving methods such as operator subgoaling, macro generalization, and problem decomposition. A third direction is to evaluate the proposed measure of problem difficulty with respect to other problem solving programs and human problem solvers. Finally, the most important extension to this work is the application of macros to other problem domains, and in particular the development of the paradigm of learning by searching for macro-operators.

9 Conclusions

There are several conclusions that can be drawn from this work. The first is that our current collection of weak methods is incomplete. In particular, there exists problems, such as Rubik's Cube, that cannot be solved efficiently by any of the weak methods, including means-ends analysis and heuristic search. However, these problems can be solved by people with no prior knowledge of the problems. This implies that some other technique must be involved.

The Macro Problem Solver, a new problem solving method based on macro-operators, can solve these problems efficiently. The basic idea is that while the primitive operators of the space may make large global changes in the state of the problem, there exist sequences of primitive operators that make only small local changes. While a fairly general method, the technique depends on problem dependent knowledge in the form of the macro-operators.

These macros can be learned automatically. Learning is accomplished by searching through the space of all macro-operators for those macros which leave most of the problem state invariant. The macro learning techniques are relatively problem independent. For difficult problems, such as the full 3x3x3 Rubik's Cube, the learning methods are sufficiently powerful to find all necessary macros is a reasonable amount of computer time (less than 15 minutes).

The success of this paradigm is based on a structural property of problems called operator decomposability. An operator is totally decomposable if its effect on each component of a state can be expressed as a function of only that component of the state. Given an ordering of the state components, a operator is serially decomposable if its effect on each state component can be expressed as a function of only that component and any previous components in the ordering. Total decomposability is a special case of serial decomposability. The Macro Problem

Solver and the macro learning techniques are effective for any problems which are serially decomposable. Operator decomposability is a property of a problem space which allows a general strategy for solving a problem from any initial state to be based on a relatively small amount of knowledge.

The performance of this method, measured in terms of number of macros that have to be stored, learning time, and number of primitive operators for a solution, is quite acceptable when compared with problem difficulty. In particular, 1) the number of macros is a small fraction of the total number of states in the space, 2) the amount of time to learn all the macros is of the same order as would be required to solve just one instance of the problem, and 3) the worst case solution length is no more than n times the optimal solution length, where n is the number of subgoals the problem is broken down into.

Finally, it is observed that macro-operators, viewed more generally, are a useful representation for knowledge in several domains, including road navigation, theorem proving, computer programming. This suggests that the paradigm of learning by searching for macro-operators may be a fairly general learning paradigm, or in other words, a weak method for learning.

Appendix A Complete Macro Tables

A.1 Macro Table for the Fifteen Puzzle

TILE POSITION MACRO

TILE	POSITION	MACRO
0	1	UUULLL
0	2	UUULL
0	3	UUUL
0	4	UUU
0	5	UULLL
0	9	ULLL
0	13	LLL
0	6	UULL
0	7	UUL
0	8	UU
0	10	ULL
0	14	LL
0	11	UL
0	12	U
0	15	L
1	2	DDRRRDLUUULL
1	3	DDRRDLURRDLUUULL
1	4	DDRDLURRDLURRDLUUULL
1	5	DDDRRRUUULLL
1	9	DDRRRULDDRUUULLL
1	13	DRRRULDDRULDDRUUULLL
1	6	DRRRDLDRUUULLL
1	7	DRRDLDRURDLUUULL
1	8	DRDLDRURDLURRDLUUULL
1	10	DDRRURDLDRUUULLL
1	14	DRRULDDRURDLDRUUULLL
1	11	RRDLDRURDLDRUUULLL
1	12	RDLDRURDLDRURDLUUULL
1	15	DRURDLDRURDLDRUUULLL
2	3	DDRRDLUUUL

2	4	DDRDLURRDLUUUL
2	5	DDRRRULLDDRUUULL
2	9	DRRRDLULDDRUUULL
2	13	RRRDLULDDRULDDRUUULL
2	6	DDDRRUUULL
2	7	DRRDLDRUUULL
2	8	DRDLDRURDLUUUL
2	10	DDRRULDDRUUULL
2	14	DRRULDDRULDDRUUULL
2	11	DDRURDLDRUUULL
2	12	RDLDRURDLDRUUULL
2	15	DRULDDRURDLDRUUULL
3	4	DDRDLUUU
3	5	DDRRRDLULDRRUUULLL
3	9	DRRRDLULDRULLDDRUUUL
3	13	RRRDLULDRDLULDDRUUUL
3	6	DDRRULLDDRUUUL
3	7	DDDRUUUL
3	8	DRDLDRUUUL
3	10	DRRDLULDDRUUUL
3	14	RRDLULDDRULDDRUUUL
3	11	DDRULDDRUUUL
3	12	RDDLURDLDRUUUL
3	15	DRULDDRULDDRUUUL
4	5	DDRRRULLDRDLULDRRUUULL
4	9	DRRRDLULDRDLULDRRUUULL
4	13	RRRDLULDRDLLDRUULDRDLUUU
4	6	DDRRDLULDRRUUULL
4	7	DRRDDLULDRRUUULL
4	8	DDDRULURDDLUUU
4	10	DDDRUURDLULDRDLUUU
4	14	RRDLULDDDRUULDRDLUUU
4	11	DDDRUULDRDLUUU
4	12	RDLDDRUULDRDLUUU
4	15	DRULDDDRUULDRDLUUU
5	9	DDRRRUULLL
5	13	DRRRULDDRUULLL
5	6	DRRRDLUULL
5	7	DRRDLURRDLUULL
5	8	DRDLURRDLURRDLUULL
5	10	RRRDLDRUULLL
5	14	DRRURDLDRUULLL
5	11	RRDLDRURDLUULL
5	12	RDLDRURDLURRDLUULL

5	15	DRURDLDRURDLUULL
9	13	DRRRULLL
9	6	DRRDLUURRDLULL
9	7	DRDRULURRDLULL
9	8	DDRULURRDLURRDLULL
9	10	RRRDLULL
9	14	DRRURDLULL
9	11	RRDLURRDLULL
9	12	RDLURRDLURRDLULL
9	15	DRURDLURRDLULL
13	6	RRRDLDLUURDRULLL
13	7	DRDRUURDLLURDRULLL
13	8	DDRULURRRDLLURDRULLL
13	10	DRRURDLLURDRULLL
13	14	RRRDLULDRRULLL
13	11	RRRDLLURDRULLL
13	12	RDLURRRDLLURDRULLL
13	15	DRRURDLULDRRULLL
6	7	DRRDLUUL
6	8	DRDLURRDLUUL
6	10	DDRRUULL
6	14	DRRULDDRUULL
6	11	RRDLDRUULL
6	12	RDLDRURDLUUL
6	15	DRURDLDRUULL
7	8	DRDLUU
7	10	DRRULLDDRUUL
7	14	RRDLULDDRUUL
7	11	DDRUUL
7	12	RDLDRUUL
7	15	DRULDDRUUL
8	10	DRRDLULDRRUULL
8	14	DDRUURDLULDRDLUU
8	11	RRDDLULDRRUULL
8	12	DDRULURDDLUU
8	15	DDRUULDRDLUU
10	14	DRRULL
10	11	RRDLUL
10	12	RDLURRDLUL
10	15	DRURDLUL

```
14    11        DRURDLLURDRULL
14    12        RRDLLURDRULL
14    15        RRDLULDRRULL

11    12        RDLU
11    15        DRUL
```

The total number of non-identity macros is 119.
The average case solution length is 139.40 moves.

A.2 Macro Table for the 2x2x2 Rubik's Cube

CUBIE POSITION ORIENTATION MACRO

CUBIE	POSITION	ORIENTATION	MACRO					
DLF	DLF	1	F	U-	F2			
DLF	DLF	2	F2	U	F-			
DLF	DRB	0	R2	F2				
DLF	DRB	1	R	F				
DLF	DRB	2	R2	U	F-			
DLF	DRF	0	R	U	F-			
DLF	DRF	1	R	F2				
DLF	DRF	2	F					
DLF	ULB	0	U2	F2				
DLF	ULB	1	U	R-	F2			
DLF	ULB	2	U-	F-				
DLF	ULF	0	U-	F2				
DLF	ULF	1	U2	R-	F2			
DLF	ULF	2	F-					
DLF	URB	0	U	F2				
DLF	URB	1	R-	F2				
DLF	URB	2	U2	F-				
DLF	URF	0	F2					
DLF	URF	1	R-	F				
DLF	URF	2	U	F-				
DRB	DRB	1	R2	U-	R			
DRB	DRB	2	R-	U	R2			
DRB	DRF	0	R2	U	R2			
DRB	DRF	1	R-					
DRB	DRF	2	R	U-	R			
DRB	ULB	0	U2	R2				
DRB	ULB	1	U	R				
DRB	ULB	2	U2	R	U	R2		
DRB	ULF	0	U-	R2				
DRB	ULF	1	U2	R				
DRB	ULF	2	F	R2	F-			
DRB	URB	0	U	R2				
DRB	URB	1	R					
DRB	URB	2	R-	U-	R			
DRB	URF	0	R2					
DRB	URF	1	U-	R				
DRB	URF	2	R	U	R2			
DRF	DRF	1	R	F	R2	F-	U	R-
DRF	DRF	2	R	U-	F	R2	F-	R-
DRF	ULB	0	R	F-	U	F	R2	

123

DRF	ULB	1	F- U2 F
DRF	ULB	2	R U2 R-
DRF	ULF	0	R- U2 R U2 R
DRF	ULF	1	U- R U R-
DRF	ULF	2	R U- R-
DRF	URB	0	F U2 F- U2 F-
DRF	URB	1	F- U F
DRF	URB	2	U2 R U- R-
DRF	URF	0	R F R2 F- R-
DRF	URF	1	R U R-
DRF	URF	2	F- U- F
ULB	ULB	1	U- R2 U2 R- U2 R2
ULB	ULB	2	R2 U2 R U2 R2 U
ULB	ULF	0	U
ULB	ULF	1	R2 U2 R- U2 R2
ULB	ULF	2	F2 U2 F- U2 F2
ULB	URB	0	U-
ULB	URB	1	R2 U2 R U2 R2
ULB	URB	2	F2 U2 F U2 F2
ULB	URF	0	U2
ULB	URF	1	U R2 U2 R- U2 R2
ULB	URF	2	R2 U2 R U2 R2 U-
ULF	ULF	1	F R- F- U- R- U R
ULF	ULF	2	R- U- R U F R F-
ULF	URB	0	U F R U R- U- F-
ULF	URB	1	U- F- R U F U F- R-
ULF	URB	2	F U R U- R- F- U-
ULF	URF	0	R- F R U F U- F-
ULF	URF	1	R F U- F- U- R- F U
ULF	URF	2	F U F- U- R- F- R
URB	URB	1	R U2 F2 R- F- U F- U R- U
URB	URB	2	U- R U- F U- F R F2 U2 R-
URB	URF	0	U- R- U R- F2 R F- R- F2 R2
URB	URF	1	R- F- U2 F- R U R- F U2 R U-
URB	URF	2	U2 F2 U- F- U F2 U- R U- R-

The total number of non-identity macros is 75.
The average case solution length is 27.00 moves.

A.3 Macro Table for the 3x3x3 Rubik's Cube

CUBIE POSTN ORIENT MACRO

CUBIE	POSTN	ORIENT	MACRO		
UF	UL	0	L	F	
UF	UL	1	U-		
UF	UB	0	U2		
UF	UB	1	B	L	U-
UF	UR	0	R-	F-	
UF	UR	1	U		
UF	UF	1	F-	L-	U-
UF	LF	0	L-	U-	
UF	LF	1	F		
UF	LB	0	L	U-	
UF	LB	1	L2	F	
UF	RB	0	R-	U	
UF	RB	1	R2	F-	
UF	RF	0	R	U	
UF	RF	1	F-		
UF	DL	0	L-	F	
UF	DL	1	L2	U-	
UF	DB	0	D2	F2	
UF	DB	1	B-	L	U-
UF	DR	0	R	F-	
UF	DR	1	R2	U	
UF	DF	0	F2		
UF	DF	1	F	L-	U-
ULF	ULF	1	L	D-	L2
ULF	ULF	2	L2	D	L-
ULF	ULB	0	B	D	L-
ULF	ULB	2	L		
ULF	ULB	1	B	L2	
ULF	URB	0	B2	L2	
ULF	URB	1	B	L	
ULF	URB	2	R2	D-	L-
ULF	URF	0	R2	D	L2
ULF	URF	2	R2	D2	L-
ULF	URF	1	R-	D-	L-
ULF	DLF	0	D-	L2	
ULF	DLF	2	L-		
ULF	DLF	1	D2	B-	L2
ULF	DLB	0	L2		
ULF	DLB	1	B-	L	
ULF	DLB	2	D	L-	
ULF	DRB	0	D	L2	
ULF	DRB	2	D2	L-	

125

ULF	DRB	1	B- L2
ULF	DRF	0	D2 L2
ULF	DRF	1	D B- L2
ULF	DRF	2	D- L-
UL	UL	1	F2 U- F- L- F-
UL	UB	0	F B L F-
UL	UB	1	F2 U- F2
UL	UR	0	F2 U2 F2
UL	UR	1	F U F- L-
UL	LF	0	U L2 B- L2 U-
UL	LF	1	U L- U L U-
UL	LB	0	F2 B- U- F2
UL	LB	1	F L F-
UL	RB	0	L- U B U-
UL	RB	1	L D2 B2 L
UL	RF	0	F- U F
UL	RF	1	F2 L- F2
UL	DL	0	F L2 F-
UL	DL	1	L- U- F U
UL	DB	0	U B- U- L
UL	DB	1	F2 B2 U- F2
UL	DR	0	F R2 B U2
UL	DR	1	R F- U F
UL	DF	0	F L- F-
UL	DF	1	F2 U F2
LF	UB	0	U- L U
LF	UB	1	U2 F- U2
LF	UR	0	U F- U-
LF	UR	1	U2 L U2
LF	LF	1	U2 L- U- F- U-
LF	LB	0	U2 L2 U2
LF	LB	1	B- U- L U
LF	RB	0	U R2 F2 U-
LF	RB	1	B U- L U
LF	RF	0	U F2 U-
LF	RF	1	R U F- U-
LF	DL	0	U D F U-
LF	DL	1	U2 L- U2
LF	DB	0	U2 D L- U2
LF	DB	1	U D2 F U-
LF	DR	0	U D- F U-
LF	DR	1	U R F2 U-
LF	DF	0	U2 D- L- U2
LF	DF	1	U F U-

126

ULB	ULB	2	B2	D	B-			
ULB	ULB	1	B	D-	B2			
ULB	URB	0	R	D	B-			
ULB	URB	1	R	B2				
ULB	URB	2	B					
ULB	URF	0	R2	B2				
ULB	URF	2	R2	D	B-			
ULB	URF	1	R	B				
ULB	DLF	0	D2	B2				
ULB	DLF	2	D-	B-				
ULB	DLF	1	D	R-	B2			
ULB	DLB	0	D-	B2				
ULB	DLB	1	D2	R-	B2			
ULB	DLB	2	B-					
ULB	DRB	0	B2					
ULB	DRB	2	D	B-				
ULB	DRB	1	R-	B				
ULB	DRF	0	D	B2				
ULB	DRF	1	R-	B2				
ULB	DRF	2	D2	B-				
UB	UB	1	L	B2	L2	D	L	B-
UB	UR	0	L	R	B	L-		
UB	UR	1	B2	R2	D	R2	B2	
UB	LB	0	U-	F	L	F-	U	
UB	LB	1	U	R	U-	D	B-	
UB	RB	0	R2	B-	U	R	U-	
UB	RB	1	L	B	L-			
UB	RF	0	B-	U	R	U-		
UB	RF	1	B	D2	R2	B		
UB	DL	0	L	B-	L-			
UB	DL	1	D-	L	B2	L-		
UB	DB	0	L	B2	L-			
UB	DB	1	D	L	B-	L-		
UB	DR	0	U	R-	U-	B		
UB	DR	1	D	L	B2	L-		
UB	DF	0	D2	L	B2	L-		
UB	DF	1	D-	L	B-	L-		
LB	UR	0	U-	B	U			
LB	UR	1	R	U-	B2	U		
LB	LB	1	U-	B	L-	D	L	U
LB	RB	0	U-	B2	U			
LB	RB	1	R-	U-	B	U		
LB	RF	0	R2	U-	B2	U		
LB	RF	1	R	U-	B	U		
LB	DL	0	U-	D-	B-	U		

```
LB      DL      1    B2 D2 R-  D2 B2
LB      DB      0    U2 L-  D   L   U2
LB      DB      1    U-  B-  U
LB      DR      0    U-  D   B-  U
LB      DR      1    R-  U-  B2 U
LB      DF      0    L-  B-  D-  B    L
LB      DF      1    U-  D2 B-  U

URF     URB     0    R2 D   R2
URF     URB     1    R-
URF     URB     2    R   D-  R
URF     URF     2    R-  D   R2
URF     URF     1    R2 D-  R
URF     DLF     0    D2 R2
URF     DLF     2    D2 F   D-  F-
URF     DLF     1    D   R
URF     DLB     0    D-  R2
URF     DLB     1    D2 R
URF     DLB     2    F   D2 F-
URF     DRB     0    R2
URF     DRB     2    F   D-  F-
URF     DRB     1    D-  R
URF     DRF     0    D   R2
URF     DRF     1    R
URF     DRF     2    R-  D-  R

UR      UR      1    F-  R2 F2 D-  F-  R
UR      RB      0    R   D-  R-  F-  R    F
UR      RB      1    F-  R-  F
UR      RF      0    U   L-  F-  L    U-
UR      RF      1    R2 D-  R-  F    D-  F-
UR      DL      0    D2 F-  R2 F
UR      DL      1    D   F-  R    F
UR      DB      0    D2 F-  R    F
UR      DB      1    D-  F-  R2 F
UR      DR      0    F-  R2 F
UR      DR      1    D-  F-  R    F
UR      DF      0    F-  R    F
UR      DF      1    D   F-  R2 F

URB     URB     1    B-  D   L-  D2 L    B
URB     URB     2    B-  L-  D2 L    D-  B
URB     DLF     0    R   F-  R    F    R2
URB     DLF     2    R   D2 R-
URB     DLF     1    B-  D2 B
URB     DLB     0    D-  R2 D    R2 D-  R2
URB     DLB     1    D   B-  D2 B
```

128

URB	DLB	2	R	D-	R-					
URB	DRB	0	R2	D	R2	D-	R2			
URB	DRB	2	B-	D-	B					
URB	DRB	1	R	D	R-					
URB	DRF	0	D	R2	D	R2	D-	R2		
URB	DRF	1	B-	D	B					
URB	DRF	2	D2	R	D-	R-				
RF	RB	0	R2	D2	R2	D2	R2			
RF	RB	1	R-	F-	R-	F	D	R		
RF	RF	1	F-	D-	L-	U-	R2	F	R	U L
RF	DL	0	R-	D	R	D	F	D-	F-	
RF	DL	1	R2	D2	R-	D2	R2			
RF	DB	0	D	R2	D2	R-	D2	R2		
RF	DB	1	B2	R2	D2	B-	D2	R2	B2	
RF	DR	0	R-	D2	R	D2	F	D	F-	
RF	DR	1	R2	D2	R	D2	R2			
RF	DF	0	D-	R2	D2	R-	D2	R2		
RF	DF	1	B2	R2	D2	B	D2	R2	B2	
RB	RB	1	R2	D2	B	R2	B-	D2	R-	D R-
RB	DL	0	R	D	R-	D-	B-	D-	B	
RB	DL	1	R-	D2	F-	R2	F	D2	R	
RB	DB	0	B-	D2	B	D2	R	D	R-	
RB	DB	1	B	D2	L	B	L-	D2	B-	
RB	DR	0	R	D2	R-	D2	B-	D-	B	
RB	DR	1	B	D2	L	B-	L-	D2	B-	
RB	DF	0	B-	D	B	D	R	D-	R-	
RB	DF	1	B	D2	L	B2	L-	D2	B-	
DF	DL	0	F	D	L	D-	L-	F-		
DF	DL	1	D							
DF	DB	0	D2							
DF	DB	1	B	D	R	D-	R-	B-		
DF	DR	0	R	F	D	F-	D-	R-		
DF	DR	1	D-							
DF	DF	1	R	D	F	D-	F-	R-	D-	
DL	DL	1	L-	F-	D-	F	D	L	D-	
DL	DB	0	L	D	B	D-	B-	L-		
DL	DB	1	R-	B-	D-	B	D	R		
DL	DR	0	R-	D2	R	D	R-	D	R	
DL	DR	1	R-	D-	B-	D	B	R		
DB	DB	1	R-	D-	R2	F-	R-	F2	D-	F- D2
DB	DR	0	D	B	R	D	R-	D-	B-	L D B D- B- L-
DB	DR	1	D	R	D	R-	D	R	D2	R-

```
DLF    DLF    2    R-  D-  R   D-  R-  D2 R   L   D   L · D   L   D2 L-
DLF    DLF    1    L   D2  L-  D-  L   D-  L-  R-  D2 R   D   R-  D   R
DLF    DLB    0    L   B   L-  F   L   B-  L-  F-
DLF    DLB    1    L-  F-  R   F   L   F-  R-  F
DLF    DLB    2    F   L2  F   R2  F-  L2  F   R2  F2
DLF    DRB    0    L2  B2  L   F   L-  B2  L   F-  L
DLF    DRB    2    F   L   F-  R   F   L-  F-  R-
DLF    DRB    1    F-  R   F   L-  F-  R-  F   L
DLF    DRF    0    F-  R-  F   L-  F-  R   F   L
DLF    DRF    1    L   D2  L   U   L-  D2  L   U-  L2
DLF    DRF    2    F   L   B   L-  F-  L   B-  L-

DLB    DLB    1    D-  B-  D   F   D-  B   D   L   B   L-  F-  L   B-  L-
DLB    DLB    2    L   B   L-  F   L   B-  L-  D-  B-  D   F-  D-  B   D
DLB    DRB    0    F   L-  F-  R   F   L   F-  R-
DLB    DRB    2    L   B2  L   F2  L-  B2  L   F2  L2
DLB    DRB    1    R-  D   L   D-  R   D   L-  D-
DLB    DRF    0    L2  F2  L-  B2  L   F2  L-  B2  L-
DLB    DRF    1    R   F   L-  F-  R-  F   L   F-
DLB    DRF    2    D   L   D-  R-  D   L-  D-  R

DRB    DRB    2    L-  D-  L   D-  L-  D2 L   R   D   R-  D   R   D2 R-
DRB    DRB    1    R   D2  R-  D-  R   D-  R-  L-  D2  L   D   L-  D   L
```

The total number of non-identity macros is 238.
The average case solution length is 86.38 moves.

A.4 Macro table for the 2x2x2 Rubik's Cube Based on Random Intermediate States

	URF	ULF	ULB	URB	DLF	DRF	DRB
1	DLF 1						
2	DRF 0	DRB 1					
3	DRB 2	ULF 0	URF 0				
4	URF 2	DRF 2	ULB 1	ULF 0			
5	URF 0	ULF 1	DRB 2	ULB 2	DLF 2		
6	URF 0	ULF 0	ULB 0	URB 0	DLF 0	DRF 0	DRB 0

CUBIE POSITION ORIENTATION MACRO

CUBIE	POSITION	ORIENTATION	MACRO
URF	DLF	0	F2 U F-
URF	DLF	2	F U- F2
URF	DRB	0	R2 U F-
URF	DRB	1	R2 F2
URF	DRB	2	R F
URF	DRF	0	F
URF	DRF	1	R U F-
URF	DRF	2	R F2
URF	ULB	0	U- F-
URF	ULB	1	U2 F2
URF	ULB	2	U R- F2
URF	ULF	0	F-
URF	ULF	1	U- F2
URF	ULF	2	F U F-
URF	URB	0	U2 F-
URF	URB	1	U F2
URF	URB	2	R- F2
URF	URF	0	U F-
URF	URF	1	F2
URF	URF	2	R- F
ULF	DRB	0	U R- U R2 F-
ULF	DRB	1	F
ULF	DRB	2	U R2 U- R F-
ULF	DRF	0	U F U2 F2 R2
ULF	DRF	1	U R2 U R2 F-
ULF	DRF	2	R- F-
ULF	ULB	0	U2 F R- F2
ULF	ULB	1	F U2 R2
ULF	ULB	2	U R F-
ULF	ULF	0	F R2 F2

ULF	ULF	1	U-	R2	F-				
ULF	ULF	2	U2	R	F-				
ULF	URB	0	U	F	R-	F2			
ULF	URB	1	U	R2	F-				
ULF	URB	2	R	F-					
ULF	URF	0	F	R-	F2				
ULF	URF	1	R2	F-					
ULF	URF	2	U-	R	F-				
ULB	DLF	0	R-	U	F-	U-	F-		
ULB	DLF	1	R-	F	U2	F	U		
ULB	DLF	2	R2	F-	R				
ULB	ULB	0	U-	R-	U2	F	U		
ULB	ULB	1	F	R	F-	U	R-		
ULB	ULB	2	F2	U2	R	F-	U		
ULB	ULF	0	R-	U2	F	U			
ULB	ULF	1	R-	F-	R-	F-	R		
ULB	ULF	2	U-	F	R2	F-	R-		
ULB	URB	0	U2	R-	U2	F	U		
ULB	URB	1	R	U-	F-	U	R2		
ULB	URB	2	R2	F2	R	F			
ULB	URF	0	U	R-	U2	F	U		
ULB	URF	1	F2	R-	F2	R-	F-		
ULB	URF	2	F	R2	F-	R-			
URB	DLF	0	R-	U-	F2	U2	F-	U-	
URB	DLF	1	R2	U	R-	U-	R	F	R-
URB	DLF	2	R	F-	R2	F2	R-	U	
URB	DRF	0	U-	F2	R2	U2	F-	U2	
URB	DRF	1	F-	R2	U2	F2	R-	U2	
URB	DRF	2	R2	U	R-	F	U-	F	R-
URB	ULB	0	R	U-	R	F-	R-	F	
URB	ULB	1	R-	U-	F2	R	U2	F-	U-
URB	ULB	2	R-	F	U-	F	U	R-	
URB	URB	0	R-	F	R2	F	U	F-	R
URB	URB	1	R2	U2	R	U2	R2	U-	R2
URB	URB	2	R-	U-	F2	R-	U2	F-	U-
DLF	DLF	0	U-	R-	F	R2	U-	F2	U2
DLF	DLF	1	F-	U2	F-	U2	R	U-	F-	U-
DLF	DLF	2	U-	F-	U	F2	R	F-	R
DLF	DRB	0	R-	F	R2	U2	F	R-	U-
DLF	DRB	1	U	F-	R-	U	R-	U2	R	F2
DLF	DRB	2	R2	U-	F	R-	U-	R2	F	R	U2
DLF	URB	0	U2	F	U	F2	U	F	U	R
DLF	URB	1	F	U2	F-	R	U2	R	U-
DLF	URB	2	R	U2	R-	U	F2	U-	R2	U-

```
DRF     DRF     0       U  F- U2 R  F  U2 F  U
DRF     DRF     1       F- U  F2 R- F  U- R2 F
DRF     DRF     2       U2 R  F- R- U  F  U- R2 F2 U2
DRF     URB     0       F- R- F2 R  F2 U- R- F  U-
DRF     URB     1       R- F2 R  F2 U2 R  U- F2 U
DRF     URB     2       F- U2 R- U- R- F2 R- F2
```

Total number of non-identity macros is 80.
Average case solution length is 32.83 moves.

A.5 Macro Table for 2x2x2 Rubik's Cube Separating Position and Orientation

CUBIE	POSITION	ORIENTATION	MACRO
DLF	DRB		R2 F2
DLF	DRF		F
DLF	ULB		U- F-
DLF	ULF		F-
DLF	URB		U2 F-
DLF	URF		F2
DLF		1	F U- F2
DLF		2	F2 U F-
DRB	DRF		R-
DRB	ULB		U2 R2
DRB	ULF		U- R2
DRB	URB		R
DRB	URF		R2
DRB		1	R2 U- R
DRB		2	R- U R2
DRF	ULB		R U2 R-
DRF	ULF		R U- R-
DRF	URB		F- U F
DRF	URF		R U R-
DRF		1	R F R2 F- U R-
DRF		2	R U- F R2 F- R-
ULB	ULF		U
ULB	URB		U-
ULB	URF		U2
ULB		1	U- R2 U2 R- U2 R2
ULB		2	R2 U2 R U2 R2 U
ULF	URB		F U R U- R- F- U-
ULF	URF		F U F- U- R- F- R
ULF		1	F R- F- U- R- U R
ULF		2	R- U- R U F R F-
URB	URF		U2 F2 U- F- U F2 U- R U- R-

```
URB                       1        R  U2 F2 R- F- U  F- U  R- U
URB                       2        U- R  U- F  U- F  R  F2 U2 R-
```

Total number of non-identity macros is 33.
Average case solution length is 38.60 moves.

A.6 Macro Table for Decomposed 3x3x3 Rubik's Cube

CUBIE POSTN ORIENT MACRO

CUBIE	POSTN	ORIENT	MACRO		
UF	UL	0	L	F	
UF	UL	1	U-		
UF	UB	0	U2		
UF	UB	1	B	L	U-
UF	UR	0	R-	F-	
UF	UR	1	U		
UF	UF	1	F-	L-	U-
UF	LF	0	L-	U-	
UF	LF	1	F		
UF	LB	0	L	U-	
UF	LB	1	L2	F	
UF	RB	0	R-	U	
UF	RB	1	R2	F-	
UF	RF	0	R	U	
UF	RF	1	F-		
UF	DL	0	L-	F	
UF	DL	1	L2	U-	
UF	DB	0	D2	F2	
UF	DB	1	B-	L	U-
UF	DR	0	R	F-	
UF	DR	1	R2	U	
UF	DF	0	F2		
UF	DF	1	F	L-	U-
ULF	ULF	1	L	D-	L2
ULF	ULF	2	L2	D	L-
ULF	ULB	0	B	D	L-
ULF	ULB	2	L		
ULF	ULB	1	B	L2	
ULF	URB	0	B2	L2	
ULF	URB	1	B	L	
ULF	URB	2	R2	D-	L-
ULF	URF	0	R2	D	L2
ULF	URF	2	R2	D2	L-
ULF	URF	1	R-	D-	L-
ULF	DLF	0	D-	L2	
ULF	DLF	2	L-		
ULF	DLF	1	D2	B-	L2
ULF	DLB	0	L2		
ULF	DLB	1	B-	L	
ULF	DLB	2	D	L-	
ULF	DRB	0	D	L2	
ULF	DRB	2	D2	L-	

ULF	DRB	1	B-	L2			
ULF	DRF	0	D2	L2			
ULF	DRF	1	D	B-	L2		
ULF	DRF	2	D-	L-			
UL	UL	1	F2	U-	F-	L-	F-
UL	UB	0	F	B	L	F-	
UL	UB	1	F2	U-	F2		
UL	UR	0	F2	U2	F2		
UL	UR	1	F	U	F-	L-	
UL	LF	0	U	L2	B-	L2	U-
UL	LF	1	U	L-	U	L	U-
UL	LB	0	F2	B-	U-	F2	
UL	LB	1	F	L	F-		
UL	RB	0	L-	U	B	U-	
UL	RB	1	L	D2	B2	L	
UL	RF	0	F-	U	F		
UL	RF	1	F2	L-	F2		
UL	DL	0	F	L2	F-		
UL	DL	1	L-	U-	F	U	
UL	DB	0	U	B-	U-	L	
UL	DB	1	F2	B2	U-	F2	
UL	DR	0	F	R2	B	U2	
UL	DR	1	R	F-	U	F	
UL	DF	0	F	L-	F-		
UL	DF	1	F2	U	F2		
LF	UB	0	U-	L	U		
LF	UB	1	U2	F-	U2		
LF	UR	0	U	F-	U-		
LF	UR	1	U2	L	U2		
LF	LF	1	U2	L-	U-	F-	U-
LF	LB	0	U2	L2	U2		
LF	LB	1	B-	U-	L	U	
LF	RB	0	U	R2	F2	U-	
LF	RB	1	B	U-	L	U	
LF	RF	0	U	F2	U-		
LF	RF	1	R	U	F-	U-	
LF	DL	0	U	D	F	U-	
LF	DL	1	U2	L-	U2		
LF	DB	0	U2	D	L-	U2	
LF	DB	1	U	D2	F	U-	
LF	DR	0	U	D-	F	U-	
LF	DR	1	U	R	F2	U-	
LF	DF	0	U2	D-	L-	U2	
LF	DF	1	U	F	U-		

ULB	ULB	2	B2	D	B-				
ULB	ULB	1	B	D-	B2				
ULB	URB	0	R	D	B-				
ULB	URB	1	R	B2					
ULB	URB	2	B						
ULB	URF	0	R2	B2					
ULB	URF	2	R2	D	B-				
ULB	URF	1	R	B					
ULB	DLF	0	D2	B2					
ULB	DLF	2	D-	B-					
ULB	DLF	1	D	R-	B2				
ULB	DLB	0	D-	B2					
ULB	DLB	1	D2	R-	B2				
ULB	DLB	2	B-						
ULB	DRB	0	B2						
ULB	DRB	2	D	B-					
ULB	DRB	1	R-	B					
ULB	DRF	0	D	B2					
ULB	DRF	1	R-	B2					
ULB	DRF	2	D2	B-					
UB	UB	1	B2	D-	R-	D2	B2	D-	B-
UB	UR	0	R-	B	D2	R2	B		
UB	UR	1	B2	R2	D	R2	B2		
UB	LB	0	B2	R	D	R	B-	D2	B-
UB	LB	1	B-	R2	B	D2	B-		
UB	RB	0	R	B	D	B-	D-	B-	
UB	RB	1	R2	B	D2	R2	B		
UB	RF	0	B2	R-	D	R	B2		
UB	RF	1	B	D2	R2	B			
UB	DL	0	D-	B	D-	R	D	B2	
UB	DL	1	D-	B-	R2	D2	B-		
UB	DB	0	B-	R2	D2	B-			
UB	DB	1	B	D-	R	D	B2		
UB	DR	0	R	B	D2	R2	B		
UB	DR	1	D	B-	R2	D2	B-		
UB	DF	0	D2	B-	R2	D2	B-		
UB	DF	1	B2	D	B	R-	B		
LB	UR	0	R-	B2	R-	B-	D	B-	
LB	UR	1	B	D-	B	R	B2		
LB	LB	1	B2	R-	B2	R2	B	D	B-
LB	RB	0	B2	D2	B2	D2	B2		
LB	RB	1	R2	B2	R-	B-	D	B-	
LB	RF	0	B2	D	R2	D-	B2		
LB	RF	1	B2	R-	B-	D	B-		
LB	DL	0	B2	D-	B	D	B2		

```
LB     DL     1     B2 D2 R-  D2 B2
LB     DB     0     D2 B2 D   R-  D-  B2
LB     DB     1     B2 D2 B-  D2 B2
LB     DR     0     R  B2 R-  B-  D   B-
LB     DR     1     B-  R-  B   R   B
LB     DF     0     B2 D   R-  D-  B2
LB     DF     1     B2 D2 B   D2 B2

URF    URB    0     R2 D   R2
URF    URB    1     R-
URF    URB    2     R   D-  R
URF    URF    2     R-  D   R2
URF    URF    1     R2 D-  R
URF    DLF    0     D2 R2
URF    DLF    2     D2 R   D   R2
URF    DLF    1     D   R
URF    DLB    0     D-  R2
URF    DLB    1     D2 R
URF    DLB    2     B   R2 B-
URF    DRB    0     R2
URF    DRB    2     R   D   R2
URF    DRB    1     D-  R
URF    DRF    0     D   R2
URF    DRF    1     R
URF    DRF    2     R-  D-  R

UR     UR     1     R  B-  R-  D2 R   D   B   R2
UR     RB     0     R  D2 R   B-  D-  B   R-
UR     RB     1     R-  D2 R-  D2 R
UR     RF     0     R-  D   R2 B   R   B-  R2
UR     RF     1     R  B-  D-  R-  D-  R   B
UR     DL     0     R-  D2 R   D2 R
UR     DL     1     R2 B-  D-  B   R-
UR     DB     0     D   R2 B-  D-  B   R-
UR     DB     1     R-  D-  R   D   R
UR     DR     0     R-  D2 R2 D2 R
UR     DR     1     D2 R2 B-  D-  B   R-
UR     DF     0     D-  R2 B-  D-  B   R-
UR     DF     1     R  B-  D   B   R2

URB    URB    1     R  B   R2 B-  D   R-
URB    URB    2     R  D-  B   R2 B-  R-
URB    DLF    0     D2 R   B   R2 B-  R-
URB    DLF    2     R  D2 R-
URB    DLF    1     B-  D2 B
URB    DLB    0     R  B   R   B-  D   R-
URB    DLB    1     D-  R   D   R-
```

```
URB    DLB    2    R    D-  R-
URB    DRB    0    R    B   R2  B-  R-
URB    DRB    2    B-   D-  B
URB    DRB    1    R    D   R-
URB    DRF    0    D    R   B   R2  B-  R-
URB    DRF    1    B-   D   B
URB    DRF    2    D2   R   D-  R-

RF     RB     0    R2   D2  R2  D2  R2
RF     RB     1    R    D   B   R-  B-  R-
RF     RF     1    R-   B-  R-  D2  R   D   B   D   R2
RF     DL     0    D    R   D2  B   R-  B-  D2  R-
RF     DL     1    R2   D2  R-  D2  R2
RF     DB     0    D    R2  D2  R-  D2  R2
RF     DB     1    B    R2  D   R2  D-  R2  B-
RF     DR     0    R-   D2  B-  D   B   D2  R
RF     DR     1    R2   D2  R   D2  R2
RF     DF     0    D-   R2  D2  R-  D2  R2
RF     DF     1    R    D2  B   R-  B-  D2  R-

RB     RB     1    R2   D2  B   R2  B-  D2  R-  D   R-
RB     DL     0    R    D   R-  D-  B-  D-  B
RB     DL     1    D    B-  D   B   D   R   D-  R-
RB     DB     0    B-   D2  B   D2  R   D   R-
RB     DB     1    D    R   D-  R-  B   R-  B-  R
RB     DR     0    R    D2  R-  D2  B-  D-  B
RB     DR     1    D-   B-  D   B   D   R   D-  R-
RB     DF     0    B-   D   B   D   R   D-  R-
RB     DF     1    D-   R   D-  R-  B   R-  B-  R

DF     DL     0    R-   B-  D-  B   D   R   D-
DF     DL     1    D
DF     DB     0    D2
DF     DB     1    B    D   R   D-  R-  B-
DF     DR     0    D    B   D   R   D-  R-  B-
DF     DR     1    D-
DF     DF     1    B    R   D   R-  D-  B-  D2

DL     DL     1    D2   R-  B-  D-  B   D   R   D
DL     DB     0    B    D   R   D-  R-  B-  D-
DL     DB     1    R-   B-  D-  B   D   R
DL     DR     0    R-   D2  R   D   R-  D   R
DL     DR     1    R-   D-  B-  D   B   R

DB     DB     1    D    B-  D-  B2  R-  B-  R2  D-  R-  D
DB     DR     0    B    D   R   D-  R-  B2  D-  B   D-  B-  D2  B   D-
DB     DR     1    D    R   D   R-  D   R   D2  R-
```

140

```
DLF    DLF    2    D   B   R-  D   R   D   B-  R-  D   B   D   B-  R   D
DLF    DLF    1    D-  R-  B   D-  B-  D-  R   B   D-  R-  D-  R   B-  D-
DLF    DLB    0    D-  R-  D-  R   B   R-  D   R   D-  B-  D2
DLF    DLB    1    R-  D-  R   B   R-  D   R   D-  B-  D
DLF    DLB    2    R   B   R-  D2  R   B-  R-  B   D2  B-
DLF    DRB    0    B   D2  B-  R   B   R-  D2  R   B-  R-
DLF    DRB    2    D   R-  D-  B   D   B-  R   B   D-  B-
DLF    DRB    1    D-  B   D   R-  D-  R   B-  R-  D   R
DLF    DRF    0    D   B   D   R-  D-  R   B-  R-  D   R   D2
DLF    DRF    1    R-  B   D2  B-  R   B   R-  D2  R   B-
DLF    DRF    2    B   D   B-  R-  B   D-  B-  D   R   D-

DLB    DLB    1    D   R   D-  B   D2  B-  R-  D2  R   D-  B   D   B-  D2  R-
DLB    DLB    2    R   D2  B   D-  B-  D   R-  D2  R   B   D2  B-  D   R-  D-
DLB    DRB    0    R-  D-  B   D   B-  R   B   D-  B-  D
DLB    DRB    2    D   R   B   R-  D2  R   B-  R-  B   D2  B-  D-
DLB    DRB    1    D   R-  D-  R   B   R-  D   R   D-  B-
DLB    DRF    0    D   B   D2  B-  R   B   R-  D2  R   B-  R-  D-
DLB    DRF    1    D-  B   D   B-  R-  B   D-  B-  D   R
DLB    DRF    2    B   D-  B-  D   R-  D-  B   D   B-  R

DRB    DRB    2    D   R2  D-  B-  R2  B   R-  D   R   D-  R2  B-  R   B   R-
DRB    DRB    1    R   B-  R-  B   R2  D   R-  D-  R   B-  R2  B   D   R2  D-
```

The total number of non-identity macros is 238.
The average case solution length is 95.31 moves.

References

[Amarel 68]   Amarel, S.
On the representations of problems of reasoning about actions.
In D. Michie (editor), *Machine Intelligence*. American Elsevier,
    New York, 1968.

[Bandelow 82]   Bandelow, Christopher.
Inside Rubik's Cube and Beyond.
Birkhauser, Boston, 1982.
translated by Jeannette Zehnder and Lucy Moser.

[Banerji 80]   Banerji, Ranan B.
Artificial Intelligence: A Theoretical Approach.
North Holland, New York, 1980.

[Banerji 83]   Banerji, Ranan B.
GPS and the psychology of the Rubik cubist: A study in
    reasoning about actions.
In A. Elithorn and R. Banerji (editors), *Artificial and Human
    Intelligence*. North-Holland, Amsterdam, 1983.

[Dawson 77]   Dawson, Clive, and Laurent Siklossy.
The role of preprocessing in problem solving systems.
In *IJCAI-5*, pages 465-471. International Joint Conference on
    Artificial Intelligence, Cambridge, Ma., August, 1977.

[Driscoll 83]   Driscoll, James R., and Merrick L. Furst.
On the diameter of permutation groups.
In *Proceedings of the 15th ACM Symposium on Theory of
    Computing*. Association for Computing Machinery, Boston,
    April, 1983.

[Elliot 82]   Elliot, R.J., and M.E. Lesk.
Route finding in street maps by computers and people.
In *Proceedings of the National Conference on Artificial
    Intelligence*, pages 258-261. American Association for
    Artificial Intelligence, Pittsburgh, Pa., August, 1982.

[Ericsson 76]   K. Anders Ericsson.
                    *Approaches to Descriptions and Analysis of Problem Solving
                        Processes: The 8-puzzle.*
                    PhD thesis, University of Stockholm, March, 1976.

[Ernst 69]   Ernst, G.W.
                    Sufficient conditions for the success of GPS.
                    Journal of the Association for Computing Machinery 16, 1969.

[Ernst 82]   Ernst, George W., and Michael M. Goldstein.
                    Mechanical discovery of classes of problem-solving strategies.
                    Journal of the Association for Computing Machinery 29(1):1-23,
                        January, 1982.

[Fikes 72]   Fikes, Richard E., Peter E. Hart, and Nils J. Nilsson.
                    Learning and executing generalized robot plans.
                    Aritificial Intelligence 3:251-288, 1972.

[Frey 82]   Frey, Alexander H. Jr., and David Singmaster.
                    Handbook of Cubik Math.
                    Enslow, Hillside, New Jersey, 1982.

[Furst 80]   Furst, Merrick, John Hopcroft, and Eugene Luks.
                    Polynomial-time algorithms for permutation groups.
                    In *21st Annual Symposium on Foundations of Computer Science*,
                        pages 36-41. IEEE, Syracuse, New York, October, 1980.

[Gaschnig 79]   Gaschnig, John.
                    *Performance Measurement and Analysis of Certain Search
                        Algorithms.*
                    PhD thesis, Department of Computer Science, Carnegie-Mellon
                        University, May, 1979.

[Goldberg 79]   Goldberg, Allen T.
                    On the Complexity of the Satisfiability Problem.
                    PhD thesis, Computer Science Department, New York University,
                        October, 1979.
                    Courant Computer Science Report #16.

[Goldstein 77]   Goldstein, M. M.
                    The mechanical discovery of problem solving strategies.
                    Report ESCI-77-1, Case Institute of Technology, Case Western
                        Reserve University, Cleveland, Ohio, 1977.

[Jerrum 82]   Jerrum, Mark.
A compact representation for permutation groups.
In *Proceedings of the 23rd Symposium on the Foundations of Computer Science*, pages 126-133. Institute of Electrical and Electronics Engineers, 1982.

[Johnson 79]   Johnson, W. A. and W. E. Storey.
Notes on the '15' puzzle.
American Journal of Mathematics 2:397-404, 1879.

[Knuth 73]   Knuth, Donald E.
The Art of Computer Programming. Volume 3: *Sorting and Searching.*
Addison-Wesley, Reading, Ma., 1973.

[Korf 80]   Korf, R. E.
Toward a model of representation changes.
Artificial Intelligence 14:41-78, 1980.

[Korf 82]   Korf, R.E.
A program that learns to solve Rubik's Cube.
In *Proceedings of the National Conference on Artificial Intelligence*, pages 164-167. Pittsburgh, Pa., August, 1982.

[Korf 83a]   Korf, R.E.
Operator decomposability: A new type of problem structure.
In *Proceedings of the National Conference on Artificial Intelligence*. Washington, D.C., August, 1983.

[Korf 83b]   Korf, R.E.
Learning to Solve Problems by Searching for Macro-Operators.
PhD thesis, Department of Computer Science, Carnegie-Mellon University, July, 1983.

[Korf 85]   Korf, R. E.
Macro-Operators: A Weak Method for Learning.
Artificial Intelligence , to appear 1985.

[Kuipers 77]   Kuipers, Benjamin Jack.
Representing Knowledge of Large-Scale Space.
PhD thesis, Artificial Intelligence Laboratory, Massachusetts Institute of Technology, July, 1977.
AI-TR-418.

[Kuipers 78]   Kuipers, Benjamin.
Modeling Spatial Knowledge.
Cognitive Science 2:129-153, 1978.

[Newell 69]   Newell, Allen.
Heuristic programming: ill-structured problems.
In J.S. Aronofsky (editor), *Progress in Operations Research*,
      chapter 10, pages 363-413. John Wiley & Sons, 1969.

[Newell 72]   Newell, A. and H. A. Simon.
Human Problem Solving.
Prentice-Hall, Englewood Cliffs, N.J., 1972.

[Newell 82]   Newell, Allen.
The knowledge level.
Artificial Intelligence 18:87-127, 1982.

[Pohl 71]   Pohl, Ira.
Bi-directional search.
In Bernard Meltzer and Donald Michie (editors), *Machine
      Intelligence*, chapter 9, pages 127-140. American Elsevier,
      New York, 1971.

[Sacerdoti 75]   Sacerdoti, Earl D.
The nonlinear nature of plans.
In *IJCAI-4*. International Joint Conference on Artificial
      Intelligence, Tbilisi, Georgia, USSR, September, 1975.

[Schofield 67]   Schofield, P.
Complete solution of the eight puzzle.
In N. L. Collins and D. Michie (editors), *Machine Intelligence*.
      American Elsevier, New York, 1967.

[Siklossy 73]   Siklossy, L., and J. Dreussi.
An efficient robot planner which generates its own procedures.
In *IJCAI-3*, pages 423-430. International Joint Conference on
      Artificial Intelligence, Stanford, Ca., August, 1973.

[Simon 69]   H. A. Simon.
The Sciences of the Artificial.
M.I.T. Press, Cambridge, Mass., 1969.

[Sims 70]   Sims, Charles C.
Computational methods in the study of permutation groups.
In John Leech (editor), *Computational Problems in Abstract
      Algebra*, pages 169-183. Pergamon Press, New York, 1970.

[Sussman 75]   Sussman, Gerald J.
                A Computer Model of Skill Acquisition.
                American Elsevier, New York, 1975.

[Tate 75]   Tate, Austin.
                Interacting goals and their use.
                In *IJCAI-4*, pages 215-218. International Joint Conference on
                    Artificial Intelligence, Tbilisi, Georgia, USSR, September,
                    1975.

[Waldinger 81] Waldinger, Richard.
                Achieving several goals simultaneously.
                In Nils Nilsson and Bonnie Webber (editor), *Readings in Artificial
                    Intelligence*, pages 250-271. Tioga Publishing Co., Palo Alto,
                    Ca., 1981.

[Warren 74]   Warren, David H.D.
                Warplan: a system for generating plans.
                technical report, Department of Artificial Intelligence, University
                    of Edinburgh, June, 1974.